Am I hallucinating or has this been the weirdest few
or the most unpleasant but off-the-scale odd.

I could be appalled but I have decided to be amused

I hope this collection of columns amuses you too.

****

22.01.15

You think doggy-doo on your shoes is bad...

2015 is not yet one month old and already I have seen the word of the year. That word is... prepare yourself..."Poonado". That is, a tornado made of poo.

A group of divers off the island of Dominica, in the Caribbean, have coined the term "poonado" to describe the herculean movement that a whale performed right in front of, and subsequently all around them.

A Canadian photographer in the group hypothesised that it was a defence mechanism on the whale's part that turned the water from an idyllic crystal clear, to something that resembled chocolate milk, so thick that they could not see their hands in front of their faces.

They had faeces on their faces. And in their mouths and eyes and in their wet suits and in places that they didn't even know they had.

The gigantic mammal was perturbed by the presence of tourists in its manor and bent its microscopic whale brain to teaching them a lesson. As lessons go, it was not very sophisticated, but who needs sophistication when you can produce enough poo to coat a battleship.

Whales can not tell divers to go away. They are restricted by not having the ability to speak. They also can not sing, despite the many meditation tapes that claim that they can.

Even One Dimension can sing better than that. One Dimension can also produce a "whirlwind of excrement", but not with the force that those divers witnessed in the newly brown Caribbean Sea.

The human interlopers into the whale's domain remained motionless in wonderment as the mammal before them pointed its head to the bottom of the sea. Thinking it was about to dive, they readied their cameras to capture the magnificent animal in its descent. Things took a turn when, rather than set off for the bottom, it let off from its bottom.

Experts say that this is normal behaviour, to rid excess weight before vigorous activity.

However, the animal remained at the surface and proceeded to defecate for what the observers described as "a startling length of time".

In what sounds like a move you might see on Strictly Come Dancing, the whale then bobbed up and down and spun in circles, spreading its discharge thoroughly around itself and the divers. It was literally dirty dancing.

Revelling in this awesome sight, rather than swimming away as fast as they could, the diving group got covered in a cake-like frosting.

They claim that when the whale left the area, perhaps for hygiene reasons, the waste washed off them and left no smell. Or at least none that they could detect. But then these are people who willingly stayed still in a thick stool soup, so their senses may not be running at maximum capacity.

It is just another insight into the wonders of nature. And another excellent reason not to get into any body of water that is not completely surrounded by tiles.

26.01.15

Making monkeys

What kind of evil terrorist mastermind could get hold of the private mobile number of the director of GCHQ, a top secret facility for listening to the chatter of jihadists and everyone else that plans to do us harm?

By what delicate means could such a coup be pulled off? Can you imagine the computing power that would be involved, to side track all the expertly installed safety barriers that would stand in their way?

Can you further imagine how it is possible, in this age of fearsome threats, that a lone wolf could get so far into the corridors of power that he is put through to the Prime Minister of the country, on his personal, most secure phone?

One man managed to pull off all these feats. A single terrifying genius broke through the firewalls and the insulation that separates the intelligence and political high command from their enemies.

How was such a thing possible? Did he have a bank of processors the size of a football pitch, with which to do battle with the government's security apparatus?

Did he have Tom Cruise dangling from a wire in a hermetically sealed command room to steal the information needed? Did Brad Pitt and George Clooney plot the scheme while at the roulette tables in Caesar's Palace?

No. The man claiming responsibility for both of these security lapses explained his actions to The Sun newspaper by stating that he had made what he called "complete monkeys" out of GCHQ by getting the mobile number of the director.

He said "what's more, I'm off my face on booze and cocaine. I had some spliff too. I've been up all night, I'm utterly wasted – hilarious.' He may think it is, but the authorities do not,. They aren't that stoned.

The Prime Minister apparently ended the call that was put through to his Blackberry when he realised it was a prank. Downing Street claim that no sensitive information was disclosed, but they would say that wouldn't they? That sounds a bit like a desperate attempt to mitigate their ineptitude.

At what point did Dave realise he was talking to an inebriate? Did he think Nigel Farage had fallen off the Dry January bandwagon and was calling to offer his support? And who put a drunk stoned man through to the PM in the first place?

Downing Street said that they take security very seriously. I would imagine that those responsible have had the error of their ways explained to them in detail and at great volume, so they may be taking it even more seriously from now on.

As for GCHQ, what of their calamitous day? A man managed to get hold of the personal mobile phone number of the head of the organisation and the PM himself. As a measure of the type of person the perpetrator is, he explained to a national newspaper that he did so after consuming a swirling cocktail of illegal mind-bending chemicals.

He can't be the brightest bulb in the box and if there is one thing the intelligence community do not appreciate, it is being made to appear unintelligent by a dim bulb.

If I were the person who was out of his head on drink and drugs when I sailed past their security, I would be expecting an early alarm call any day.

I'd plan for men in dark clothing to be abseiling down my building, to burst through my windows. I might want to leave them open, it will save on the repair bill.

The government says that lessons must be learned.

They always say that.

It must be like school in there.

03.02.15

Blowing in the wind

In any mature market for fast moving consumer goods, the players are experts that, over the years, have honed their game to sharp-elbowed perfection. Every pound is fought over and to increase one's share of it is very difficult to do.

For anything with a proven demand, the game will have been played for decades, if not centuries. The last thing that came out of the blue and was fought over afresh was the information technology sector.

The old established banks did not know quite how to deal with this new upstart and failed to get in on the ground floor. By the time they had woken up to the possibilities, the nerds had taken the lift to the penthouse, leaving the traditional banks heaving themselves up the stairs.

Youths with bad haircuts and pocket protectors for their pens, came up with ideas that looked ridiculous to financiers. Flash forward ten years and the reliable old school, stiff collar industries are beginning to look shaky, while the new boys are working in offices with slides between floors and sitting on piles of money that are so huge, they don't quite know what to do with them.

The banking racket must still be annoyed with itself for not getting into the IT industry sooner. It is perfectly understandable that they did not see the possibilities of computer games and applications, because they had nothing to compare them to. The market for such things was untested, untried and unknown.

Banks do not do well when asked to envisage and imagine. They are great at balance sheets and certitudes, so some teenager coming to them and asking for money to fund a thing that allows kids to chat to each other by typing with their thumbs must have bewildered them. So they said: "No", and then they regretted that decision just as Decca regretted not signing the Beatles.

Other than IT, it is hard to think of a completely fresh and virginal market emerging in living memory. Everything that is worth a lot of money has been traded to death and all that is left is for hugely expensive advertising to persuade people to switch brands, while the vultures pick over the bones.

There is one market that is completely different, however. One that already exists but has no major players in it at all. A market with enormous demand that is worth giant mountains of money and that is ripe for the picking, and that is the market for marijuana.

Do you know how much the worldwide trade in marijuana is worth? It is about two hundred billion dollars every year. That is, a "2" followed by eleven zeros. It looks like this: $200,000,000,000. I thought that I would introduce the number to you in word form, rather than just write it out numerically, as I would not have any idea how to say it, so I assumed it might fox you too.

Bankers know how to pronounce it though. They deal in these figures every day. They trade a billion this and ten billion that all the time. Sometimes they even get to say the "T" word: a trillion. Then they have to go and lie down with a cold compress and catch their breath.

Can you imagine how excited they would become if they could get in on financing a product with an enormous existing demand but without any of the economies of scale, distribution, retail and allied services and products that mark out anything else that generates so much money?

If a banker would sell a product to a person and then secretly bet that it will fail, if they would lie to a granny to get some spare change off her, if they would risk the company to make sure of their bonus, can you conceive of what they would do to get their hands on a chunk of $200,000,000,000 every year?

In America, the thin end of the wedge is prying the door open to entrepreneurs. At the moment, the finance needed to set up businesses to take advantage of the creeping legalisation of the drug is coming from private sources. This is because, while it may be legal on a state level, it is still illegal on a national one, so the banks can't touch it, by law.

They must be tearing their hair out.

Whoever gets in quick and establishes a brand or product that captures the public's imagination will be the next Bill Gates or Mark Zuckerberg. They will be someone who starts with nothing, to eventually feature on the cover of Fortune magazine, and probably Rolling Stone too.

The market for legal marijuana is a shining pot (!) of gold that is waiting for someone to come and take it. It is a product that needs no advertising or market research, and it needs no persuasion to switch brands because there aren't any. There's nothing else like it. Try finding great unexplored and untapped wealth in the soap powder market, for instance.

Already some smart people are setting the foundations of their future fortunes. A far sighted man in America has persuaded Bob Marley's estate to allow him to use the man's name to sell the stuff.

That's genius. Stoners in great numbers will want a picture of Bob on their packet of twenty. Whatever he paid will be peanuts compared to the value of establishing a recognisable brand in a market with such a huge and established recession proof demand.

Dope smokers in the states of Washington, Oregon, Alaska, Colorado and Washington DC can now do so legally, without having to ask a friendly doctor for a prescription for medical marijuana, which is reportedly about as difficult as getting a 'scrip for sleeping pills. When California joins them, the amount of money that will be begging to be taken will sky rocket and the banks will start to get itchy.

They will think: if only there was a change in the law on a national level we could get in while the business is being run by red-eyed hippies and bearded, muesli eating tree huggers. They will see that there are billions going begging that they could put to good use by awarding themselves a bonus and buying a yacht.

They will start to mention these ideas to the people in their pay - the politicians.

Washington's political elite take the money necessary to fund their billion dollar campaign budgets from the banks and their allies. Banks do not act so generously out of the kindness of their hearts, they want something in return.

It is no different here. Hence the way in which Britain's leaders were battling with the EU to protect bankers from those pesky rules that would restrict bonuses to 200% of an already gigantic salary.

When States like Arizona see how much tax money is pouring into the coffers of their dope selling neighbour states, then the floodgates in America will finally open and the clamour from Wall Street to be allowed to join the party will become deafening. And when the banks in America are earning so much new and previously untapped money, banks in this country will want to be doing the same.

The politicians' minds will be changed for them by the industry that generously offers them retirement incomes in non-jobs as directors or advisors.

The war on drugs, or at least the war on grass, will be consigned to history. Politicians will tell us it is because they have been advised that it is unwinnable, or causing to much harm, or it is diverting too many resources to combat.

Really, though, it will be because there simply is no other financial fruit that is so ripe and will be so easy to pick.

A change is going to come. It will blow in from EC1.

14.02.15

Valentine's Day, Massacred

Things just got worse for Nick Clegg. I know what you are thinking: how could that possibly happen? Is there any leeway for his luck to get less favourable before he leaves this earth to join the choir invisible?

Did he wake one morning to find his knees had been stolen? Did his ears catch fire and he tried to put them out with a pick axe? Did the party he leads become even less popular than it was before?

Yes. That last one.

It is hard to believe that the Liberal Democrats have space in which they can extend their disapproval rating but new territories are being discovered all the time and they have found storage space in the internet cloud for all the extra opprobrium they have been attracting lately.

A poll for the Evening Standard puts Nick's lot on 6% of the vote. At the last general election, they managed 23%. That figure seems so improbably high that I checked it twice. Fifty seven seats in total, and all because the undecided public saw Nick and Dave and Gordon on the telly and picked Nick because he wasn't the other two.

He seemed nice, earnest, real and trustworthy. Now all anyone says about him is that he U-turned on student course fees.

Critics talk about this as though it was the worst thing that ever happened to students in the history of education.

That is not true. The worst thing that ever happened to students, apart from the importation of Moroccan hash that was like smoking a rolled up carpet, was a British Telecom ad. You know, the one with Maureen Lipman and the grandson with the "ology".

I bet that children that saw that ad, with the lad that was too stupid to pass anything but pottery and sociology, and thought: I could do that, I could do an ology and spend the rest of my time in the students' bar.

And so they did. They are now the ones asking for spare change please and sleeping in the doorway where Dolcis used to be.

The truth about the student fees U-turn is that it has not affected the number of poorer students applying for university.

In Scotland, where it is all free, there are fewer poorer students going to uni than there are in England where it costs £9,000 a term.

And in England, it will only cost that much if they ever pay it back, which they won't unless they are earning over £21,000 a year, which seems unlikely, the way things are going, especially if they have done an ology.

23.02.14

Put Down The Spoon And Step Away From The Crumble

What can you eat that will not kill you before pudding? This is a question that Man has asked itself since the invention of eating for pleasure, which in Great Britain was around 1970. Before the seventies, eating in Britain was strictly a method of staying alive, like breathing.

In the 1960's all food was boiled to a mush and smelled like your granny. Previous to the sixties, food was scarce and so you ate what you were given. And you would sit there until you had finished it, even if it was semolina.

For the uninitiated, semolina was a combination school dinner desert and wallpaper paste which no child on earth wanted to consume. Adults used it to punish the youth when their canes had gone astray.

Then along came the Galloping Gourmet. A fellow with an exotic New Zealand accent burst across our tiny square television screens and dared to treat food with humour and a casual insouciance that seemed quite a leap from the starched, pinched, bolt upright propriety of Fanny.

His name was Graham Kerr and he performed his way through making a meal in front of a studio audience and then invited one strategically placed lovely to come up and eat it with him. The camera would zoom in on his face to see him fairly expire with pleasure as he popped what he had made into his mouth. Cue audience salivation and a desire to eat that too.

The desire was not to actually make it, just to eat it. That has not changed in forty years, despite the fact that almost every show on the thousand channels that we now get is about teaching the viewers to cook.

Once pleasure entered the kitchen, and supermarkets provided something to consume other than radishes and corned beef, we started to wonder if we could just help ourselves to any old thing we wanted without ruining our health.

The answer came from an army of experts and nutritionists, doctors, chefs, food company reps and newspapers. The answer was: NO!

Over the intervening decades we have been told that you should not eat butter – marge is better. Nor should you eat cream, full fat milk, chips, crisps, mash, anything potato-ey, anything bread-y, eggs, prawns, ham, sausages, steaks, anything that used to be part of a cow, or a pig or anything else that uses four legs to get around on.

Two legs are fine. Unless it is a penguin. We don't put penguins in our shopping baskets, even though they are already frozen.

We have been told that to maximise our chances of living a full and svelte life, we must not eat a rabbit, we should eat LIKE a rabbit. It was OK to eat anything green that did not come out of your nose, raw fish, chicken breast as often as public holidays come around, carrots and a piece of fruit on Sunday. That was about it. And a very small glass of wine (red) every other week.

We followed this advice not at all, and the nation's waistlines expanded like an oligarchs bank account. So we turned to the very companies that made us fat in the first place to make us slim. All those meals in boxes that we fed on while watching cookery shows had hidden dangers like fat. Fat makes you fat. Stands to reason.

This revelation started the low-fat industry. Let's be honest though, fat makes things taste nice, so the industry sold slimming foods to us that were fat free but loaded with sugar to make them palatable.

Our weight piled on even more.

The new thinking is that instead of avoiding butter, it is actually good for us. Same goes for full fat milk, yogurt, cheese, eggs and chocolate. In fact all the things the experts have been telling us to avoid are now the things they are telling us to eat.

Except sugar. Sugar is still the bête noir of the table, the crack cocaine of the kitchen.

Until they change their minds, the current answer to the question: "what can you eat that will not kill you before pudding?" is: anything you fancy.

Except pudding.

28.02.15

Springtime for Nigel.

The Ukip Spring get together started just as you would expect: a high kicking, goose stepping, Kugelblitz tank full of jack booted Nazis. They parked their Panzer in Margate and did the Hitler hi-how-are-you straight armed salutation to the sea front. It could not have gone any better if Albert Speer had designed the conference centre.

This followed a television programme that allowed air time to unreconstructed Ukip acolytes to express themselves in the "I'm not racist but..." manner.

This in turn followed a Facebook faux pas in which a Ukip activist's account posted messages describing Leicester as a "S***hole" and full of "P**is". The former claim is debatable, the latter somewhat impolite.

The string of missteps does not end there. A judge reprimanded a father for allowing his children to be assailed by Kipper-ish opinions. No longer should the dad allow his offspring to attend Ukip meetings for fear of "emotional damage".

Previously, a television station had imagined the nightmarish collapse of society that might ensue should Farage become our next Prime Minister.

Nigel himself has just returned from a catastrophic appearance at an American Tea Party rally where the only people who remained to watch him speak appeared to be cleaning the hall.

The press had a well practised Victorian fainting fit over the less salubrious elements of the week's Ukip stories.

It was all terrible news but none of it was UKIP's fault.

First off, the Nazi two steppers had nothing to do with Ukip, other than co-opting the publicity that their conference provided.

In the photo bomb of the year so far, a troupe of actors from the touring version of Mel Brooks' The Producers sprang Springtime For Hitler on the unsuspecting conventioneers to advertise their forthcoming show. A genius move on their part, particularly the sourcing of the tank, which they probably did not hire at Hertz.

The television programme about the real Kippers could have been made on any political party. To generate some shock horror headlines, eager documentarians need only point their cameras at a group of supporters long enough and eventually one or more of them will break ranks and taboos.

The imagining of a dystopian, riot strewn Kipper future was just a standard Channel 4 cheap shot.

The man with the wayward Facebook account says he is the victim of hacking and that the posts had nothing to do with him, and the judge who objected to a man taking his children to a political event should probably mind her own business, unless she would rule identically if the party in question had been the Conservatives, for instance.

As for Nigel's oration to an empty room, well, he was in America, where no-one has heard of him, and he was following an address by the Tea Party darling Sarah Palin, so the audience was probably outside enjoying a post orgasm cigarette, or shopping for assault rifles.

None of the lurid and gleeful headlines generated about Ukip had anything to do with them, or at the very most described conditions that are symptomatic of all parties. This knowledge, of course, did not stay the hand of the Fleet Street executioners.

There was one positive element to all this. If none of that had happened, and the press were not otherwise engaged, just think how much worse Green Party leader Natalie "Meltdown" Bennett's week would have been!

16.03.15

Where's our dinner?

Was the most important news story of the week that Boko Haram had pledged their allegiance to ISIS to create an international swivel-eyed House of Crazy? Was it that Ed Miliband has two kitchens, or three kitchens as is now alleged? Was it that North Korea has started testing it's rockets again?

No, no and no, in that order.

The most important story of the week was that a fat middle-aged man did not get his dinner.

It seems a bit weird sitting down to defend someone who is a multi millionaire and so powerful a figure in the media that a supper related incident would make the front pages for an entire week and counting, but I have a personal stake in the story. I want to see what they would have done with the remaining episodes of Top Gear.

The story, as it was initially described by a press that was practically beside itself at the news that someone as unreconstructed as Jeremy Clarkson should be about to fall, was that he had kept his transport waiting (rude), drank wine till his fuel gauge registered "full" (inebriated) and then arrived in a hotel (luxury) and demanded hot food from a meek serving staff who had to explain that the chef had gone home (Fawlty Towers style).

The details were exquisite. He was not only drinking wine but it was rose wine, which struck me as a little odd for a man so...real ale-y.

It was not a cab he had kept outside in attendance while he let it's meter tick over at the public's expense, it was a helicopter, and the dinner he was offered was a salad and specifically not an 8oz sirloin steak with pan-fried wild mushrooms, grilled cherry tomatoes, peppercorn sauce and fondant potatoes at £21.95. Definitely not chips and precisely not £22.

On a point of order Jeremy, having seen you age on my TV since you started Top Gear, and getting vivid reminders of what you used to be like by the magic of repeats on Dave, perhaps a salad every now and then wouldn't go amiss.

Since the first telling, he has sobered up, in the tale anyway. He is now reported to have been totally un-inebriated but highly stressed after a nightmare of a day filming. He did punch an underling, though. Or he didn't but there might have been pushing, or there wasn't. So that's clear.

We will find out in due course because an inquiry has been launched. They have imported a public servant grandee to oversee his trial which will deliberate over the facts before coming to a guilty verdict.

What seems odd to me is that a show that brings in over £ 50m a year to the company that puts it out should be catered for so erratically. If the filmed reports from the aerodrome where it is set are true, the team operate from a Portakabin. On location, they appear to operate out of their cars.

If a cinema film was guaranteed to bring in its production company a £50m profit I would expect there to be a catering truck at the very least. There would also be motor homes for the stars of such size and opulence that African dictators would get jealous. For a show that brings in so much cash, it seems to be a bit haphazardly provided for.

The upshot is that we, the Top Gear loving public, have had our toys taken away from us and we haven't even done anything wrong. How are we going to learn if we get punished for things that are not our fault?

The cancellation of the rest of the series seems to be on the basis that JC might not be a very nice person who might have done something that was not very nice.

The problem with that is if we we are only allowed to be amused by people who are very nice, there would be almost nothing to watch on TV. Telly people, as a whole, are arrogant, boastful, irritating and demanding (as opposed to radio people who are an unalloyed delight!).

If we were to be entertained solely by nice people there would only be Phillip Schofield and that bloke from The One Show on the box, twenty four hours a day. That would be enough to make me take up reading.

Unfortunately, there would not be anything to read as writers of books are all weird and unsocialised and as for journalists...well, they're beyond the pale and stand up comedians should, by and large, be in an institution and not allowed free reign to wander about in public.

That would leave sports, and if the public were only allowed to watch sportsmen that were nice, we would end up going to watch David Beckham playing with himself. And who wants to see that?

The stars of the various fields of entertainment have all exhibited behaviour that you would not want your mother to see. WC Fields was a grump, Mel Gibson had several meltdowns, Madonna was ruthless, Tom Cruise is from outer space and Led Zeppelin did things with fish that you wouldn't want to Google. Has anyone called for them to be banned?

Caravaggio killed someone. Are there protesters outside the National Gallery at the inclusion of his works? Are there concerned citizens inside ushering people away from viewing his paintings? No, he is regarded as one the greatest artists of all time, despite his personality crises.

The thing is, what should have been a personal moment between two people, that could have been sorted out to the satisfaction of everyone concerned, in private, has been blown up to a story so huge that you could see it from the Space Station.

Clarkson won't suffer. He has more money than God and his phone must be white hot with offers to go and punch a producer on a every rival channel on the box.

The people that are suffering are the ones that have paid for all this: us. The seven million souls who watch that show, for whom it is the couch-based highlight of the week. Not to mention the 350 million others who watch it abroad.

We, the British public, have been forced, under threat of imprisonment, to pay our TV licence, and mostly we have. We have done this on the understanding that, in return, we will be offered many amusements, of which we have selected Top Gear as among our favourites.

To have it taken away from us after we have paid for it is so deeply unfair that even rabid supporters of the BBC must be feeling the wind of change blow through their admiration of the institution.

The films have been made that would have filled the bulk of the shows' running time. Guests have been booked, including Keano "I know Kung Fu" Reeves. All that was left was to film the links in the aircraft hanger and put it on the air.

On behalf of a giant proportion of the British public, can I say that we want to see the programmes we were looking forward to and which we have already bought.

We want our TV dinner!

24.03.15

Money For Something, No Cheques For Free

If it goes on like this, pretty soon there won't be anyone left to vote for. Practically everyone who is an MP, and many who have only thought of becoming one, are currently suspended, pending an investigation into their willingness to accept money from shady sources.

The problem is that all of the political parties are in want of funds to splatter their adverts across billboards to try to persuade us that they deserve our vote.

The adverts will say something like: IF YOU DON'T VOTE FOR US, YOU'RE ALL GOING TO DIE. These adverts cost a lot of money and so the parties send their minions out to see if they can find some.

They look down the backs of their sofas, they ask for some spare change please outside the entrance to railway stations and they see how much they can get for their bodies on the open market. Not much is the answer, so the next place to look is in the pockets of the rich.

It is the money that these sources provide that greases the wheels of the political process. The parties will use it to batter the public with their opinions and promises for what will seem an eternity 'till the polls open in May.

Fortunately, when these wealthy individuals and corporations give political parties enormous sums of money, they do it out of the goodness of their hearts, without a thought for their own profit. They are just very nice people who care about democracy.

Just kidding, practically every penny that goes into the coffers of a political party is put there on the assumption that it is an investment that better pay out or there will be no more where that came from.

Essentially, British democracy is the finest system that money can buy, unless you count the American system, but the entry fee for that game is MUCH higher.

For a relatively small amount of cash – in the thousands rather than millions – you can have a party put your case, bend the law, look the other way, relax the rules and eventually give you a fancy name and a badge and stick you in the House of Lords when you feel like pretending to work for the benefit of the nation.

In there, you can burnish your reputation 'till the public forgets what grasping, venal and underhand methods you used to get that rich in the first place.

Who gives money without wanting anything in return? If you want to feel good about yourself, you buy the Big Issue, you do not bankroll political parties.

Our system is a big casino for corporations, hedge funds and the finance racket to place a small amount of their assets on red or black, or both, wait for the spin of the wheel and count their winnings.

There is another way. We can fund the major parties ourselves, out of our taxes. This would be added to our normal tax bill and would be divided up between them based on how many votes they garnered last time, or how they are faring in the polls, or how well they can hold a tune while singing in front of Simon Cowell.

Hands up who likes the idea of more taxes for funding the political parties. Thought not. So we are stuck with the process as it exists.

At least it gives the papers the opportunity to stage a sting operation to dupe some gullible MP into taking money outside of the rules, and that gives us something to reinforce our opinion that the lot of them are crooks.

You could almost count that as a win-win.

25.03.15

Helping the world by helping ourselves.

Targets. That word should come with a health warning. Targets often have the exact opposite result to that which was intended. Set a target for waiting times in Accident and Emergency, for instance, a target that states that a patient must be seen within four hours and the hospital will, on the cusp of failure, simply wheel its waiting patients into the corridor, where they are not in A & E any more.

Or they will see you within four hours but only to put you on a waiting list to get on a waiting list to be seen. When presented with a target that management's bonuses are dependent on, those managers will meet it by whatever methods they think they can get away with.

This principle was seen in the banking halls before the crisis that caused the world's economy to fall flat on its face. If you have to meet a target for selling insurance to people, you will sell to anyone that comes across your path, whether they need it, or even understand what they are buying.

If you have to meet targets to sell mortgages, you will meet the expectations of your bosses by selling a mortgage to someone who couldn't raise the money to buy a cappuccino, let alone a house.

In the short term, bankers got their bonus and kept their job, in the long term, everyone on

Earth got a little poorer. Some got a LOT poorer.

Of course, some just kept getting richer but those people have a special personal parking place waiting for them in Hell.

Your local council has a target that comes round every year. At the counting of the budget, when the financial year is up, they have to have spent all the money that was allocated to them, or they will be judged to not need so much next year.

Councils will send out teams of high visibility workpersons to stand around potholes and suck their teeth. They will dig up roads so that another team can fill them in, they will create bike lanes that are six feet long (there was one where I used to live in Wandsworth) and they will erect many signs telling you what you already knew.

All this waste is to ensure that the council has just as much money to waste in the following financial year.

Governments also have targets. They are self imposed, so they have no excuse. One such was giving 0.7% of our national income in foreign aid.

Zero point seven per cent may not sound like much but it is levelled on an amount that is so large that there are not enough zeros on this computer to write it out in full. It is 2.446 trillion US dollars, the currency that most big numbers come in.

The target to spend £11.5bn every year is somewhat taxing, as you can imagine. After you have employed your chauffeur, held a round of fact finding parties, travelled first class to other, often more clement parts of the world to see how they spend their aid budget, what are you going to use it on?

The answer is not to worry, just give it to someone else and they will spend it on your behalf. Faced with the end of the financial year looming, Britain's aid budget has been thrown at all sorts of proxy spenders of other people's money in the guise of do-goodery.

These are organisations which go out and throw money around on behalf of governments that can't be bothered to figure out what to do with it themselves.

These people are the most efficient way of wasting vast amounts of cash that has ever been devised short of setting fire to it. Or, they are the best way to distribute much needed aid to where it can do the most good. You decide.

Some examples of aid spending include £60m on a Moroccan water park, complete with golf course and a thousand villas, which was given £800,000 by EuropeAid, which is where much of British aid funds have gone.

There was also £8.35m given to an international programme to make physical education more meaningful. Whatever that means. We gave £15m to stop Columbian cows farting and £3.8m to an Ethiopian all female pop band to promote girl power.

I admit that those examples were selected to make aid spending look ridiculously wasteful, but still.

In truth, much aid money goes to the right place, and there is often not enough to help all those that deserve our assistance but how can we spend more without increasing the percentage of the national income that is ring fenced for it?

Fortunately, the amount our government has pledged to spend, whether it can think of good ways of doing so or not, has just gone up, because the nation's income has just gone up.

This is nothing to do with George Osborne. Even he would not try to take credit for it because UK income has been revised sharply upwards recently as two avenues of expenditure are now included that did not used to be.

They are drug taking and the renting of prostitutes. The two can often go hand in hand and account for so much money that you would need a bank to put it all in.

Fortunately, bankers are one of the main consumers of these products and services, so the cash does not have too far to travel.

By sticking to a strict routine of getting high and purchasing executive massages we can increase the income of the nation, which by turn increases the amount we give to those worse off.

Aid delivered, targets met, problem solved.

26.03.15

You'll always find parties in the kitchen at poll time

Kitchens are the heart of the home. The room in which you gain sustenance, chat about your day, commune with the family, post lists to do, store food, make meals, get tea.

It is the family room for families that don't have family rooms. It can be rurally aspirational, homey, organic and free range, or steely and minimal and anally retentive. The kitchen is a chaos of succulents and saucepans, or it is barren meters of polished surfaces and unused matching kettles and toasters.

It is the room which says more about who you are than the bathroom cabinet, which is why politicians like to invite us into theirs when they want to reinforce the notion that they are one of us, that they have normal lives too.

Ed Miliband invited the cameras into one of his spare kitchens. In what was described in the press as a mansion, we saw what looked like the spartan, moribund cooking area of a 1980's council flat. The main kitchen was presumably a little too grand, a little too unachievable for the core Labour voter for him to be seen in.

The ruse did not work and it doubly did not work when it was mooted that he had another kitchen for his live in staff, making three in the same house,. How un-Old Labour is that?

David Cameron opened not only his kitchen for the cameras, but his fridge too. Big mistake...huge.

The contents of his kitchen were taken apart by the papers and held up as a risible mix of faddish middle class health food wonkery and try-too-hard, loving the planet, fair tradism.

Dave buys healthful manuka honey from New Zealand, which is the stuff that costs so much it should come in Faberge containers, his salt is from the sea, and not from Saxa where everyone else gets theirs, he cooks with virgin coconut oil and uses vanilla bean paste and £14 vinegars.

Cameron keeps this stuff in a £2,000 fridge, mixes it up in a £240 food processor and cooks it on a range, while sipping espresso from his £355 coffee maker.

And when I say "his", I mean "our", as we bought the stuff by donating £30,000 to fit out the kitchen he uses above the office in Downing Street.

According to the pictures, the PM cooks and eats in a white shirt and cuff-links. He gets not a speck of food on him while he is doing it. This is not normal.

Unfazed by the ridicule, and still desperate for some in-kitchen propaganda, he allowed himself to be interviewed in there about his prospects for a third term of office.

Just weeks before going to the polls, he announced he was uninterested in running a third time after his forthcoming victory and went so far as to name a list of potential successors.

"Outrageous!", said the press. "Taking the British public for granted" huffed Labour campaign chief Douglas Alexander. "Presumptuous" said the Lib Dems.

It isn't him – it's the curse of the kitchen. Some things should be kept from the public's gaze.

Like the contents of the top drawer of your bedside table, there is too much in there that could give you away, allow your enemy ammunition and scupper your chances of a second term, never mind about a third.

After such a whipping from the press and his peers, it is handy that Dave has so much of that curative Antipodean honey to hand.

26.03.15

Top Tears

I write this from the standpoint of a fan. Top Gear is probably my favourite British TV show. I can not imagine sitting for hours watching repeats of any other programmes I have already seen with so much enjoyment. The only physical paper I buy is the Sunday Times and if Jeremy Clarkson (and A.A. Gill) left, I wouldn't bother. So what happened recently has been quite painful.

The BBC has not renewed his contract. Top Gear is over. There were signs it was petering out – the jokes were the same wherever they were filming. There was the crashing into each other's parked cars, the late night sabotaging, the buying of inappropriate gifts and so on.

It was like a band that only played their greatest hits, it almost became a tribute act to itself, so perhaps it was time to go, but it is a shame it went like this and a shame they could not have done one more encore.

What is left is the blame game. Pundits have blamed the head of BBC TV, Danny Cohen. Some blame the head of the organisation itself Tony Hall. Why couldn't these men have contained the problem and protected their asset? But it is not their fault.

The internet has froth coming out of its mouth it is so furious with the producer who was at the centre of the storm. The amount of unhinged vitriol that Oisin Tymon has had directed at him is depressingly predictable. If it was paint you could shellac a cathedral with it. But it is not his fault either.

If you advertised his position as a producer on Top Gear, there would be a queue of prospective candidates that would stretch to 1978. Why would he want to lose such a great job? He did not ask for all this attention and he can't be enjoying any of it.

The people who, hiding behind the anonymity of the net, have bravely called for him to curl up and die and who are haranguing his family ought to be made to repeat those bug-eyed outpourings on a soap box in the middle of their High Street on a Saturday afternoon. I doubt they would be so courageous.

The internet troglodytes blame the producer. He is such a coward, said one. He should be ashamed of himself, said another. Those were the printable ones. This is the sound of babies who have had their dummies taken away. It is an arm flailing, hissy fit of childish pique and misses the target by a good few feet.

Jeremy Clarkson blamed the BBC. "The BBC have f***ed themselves". "It was a great show and they f***ed it up", he said.

Close, but no cigar. It WAS a great show, but it was not the BBC that f***ed it up, it was one J. Clarkson that did that.

After a moment of reflection, I imagine he will write that it was indeed all his fault and that he is very sorry. His future acceptance by a large part of the public might hinge on that. At the moment though, it looks like the blaming of everyone except the person whose fault it actually is.

Uncomfortably, this sounds like the actions of a playground bully – acting the tough guy until you get caught, then saying that someone else did it.

Compare and contrast that with Stephen Gerrard's instant mea culpa after being sent off at Anfield this week. No excuses, took the blame, begged forgiveness.

Now we know that Clarkson shouted at a defenceless underling for twenty minutes (twenty!) and then split his lip because he couldn't have his choice of entrées, it rather sours the J.C. brand.

All that on-screen name calling and practical jokery at his co-presenters' expense now has a less pleasant ring to it. It might not seem so funny when we watch the repeats because of what we now know of the man.

Have you ever shouted at someone who couldn't fight back for twenty minutes in your whole life? Me neither. Who does?

I suspect that his bravado since the incident, in name calling of the BBC, in saying that he had been sacked already, was in the knowledge that his actions had painted them into a corner. What he did left them no option.

It was not Danny Cohen or Tony Hall or Oisin Tymon that killed Top Gear. It was the man who made it in the first place. I am a big fan of his work but, based on the evidence we have heard over the past few weeks, I am not such a big fan of the man any more.

I'm with James May – he does appear to be a bit of a knob.

30.03.15

It's a stick up

You've just had pay day and already you don't have any money. The reason for that is that:
A) you are an out of control spendthrift, or
B) the government took it all away and called it taxes.

Taxes are what we pay to live in an ordered society. Taxes pay for street lighting, rubbish collection, security and chocolate.

That's right, the government has taken the money it collects from you that you thought went to schooling the nation's children and used it to make them fat.

Incredibly, £637,812 was given to Cadbury's for what is called "confectionery production". This sum was gifted to one of the biggest companies on earth to help them in their core business.

I checked, Cadbury's parent company makes $35bn in sales every year. Thirty-five billion dollars!

They will notice that £637,812 like we would notice losing the spare change we keep in the car's ashtray to the mechanic who does its MOT.

We also gave £356,076 to the not inconsiderably wealthy Pepsico company to research dehydrated snacks. I'm feeling dehydrated just thinking about it.

Pepsico made $38.33bn gross profit in the last financial year. I would imagine that they could afford to research snacks using their own money, but why would they want to when they can use ours instead?

Nestle, the makers of...well, practically everything in your cupboard, were gifted £487,268 to look into chocolate cooling technology. I could have done that for a tenner. You leave it in a place away from the heat, it cools. Nestle's net profit last year was £6.68bn.

The whole world's gone mad.

There was, by the way, a series of other five or six figure pledges for the likes of perfecting wafer biscuits, chocolate blending and ice cream making.

Seven in ten adults in the UK are overweight. It is just a guess on my part but I don't think that these grants are helping.

These weirdly precise sums were presented to these multi-national corporations by what used to be called the Government's Technology Strategy Board. They now call themselves Innovate UK.

If I were them, I would change my name to something even less memorable and move into a teepee up a Welsh hillside where furious tax payers couldn't find me.

It used to be that the foreign aid that disappeared into African dictators' pockets and got spent on Parisian mansions, epaulettes and Ray-Ban sunglasses was the quickest way to get rid of all that pesky taxpayers' cash that lays about the place in Westminster.

Well, there's a new entrant in the race to disappear all our money.

Is my memory playing tricks on me, or did The Milky Bar kid used to dress like a bandit?

02.04.15

On the cusp of something BIG

There has been a lot of uninformed speculation about what the Top Gear men will do next. Allow me to add my own uninformed speculation here.

Commentators have called it the end of an era, that the format is bigger than the stars, that they are doomed to eke out the rest of their lives as a shadow of their former, popular selves.

I suspect that their future lies on a different path. I do not see them as being a spent force that will die a slow death on a commercial channel.

I think that they will do a "Howerd Stern".

Howerd Stern is an American radio talk show host. The content of his programmes is to British radio talk shows as Debbie Does Dallas is to Blue Peter.

Stern is an arch controversialist that has been delighting his young American audience for decades with features such as "Bestiality Dial -a-Date", "Who's the Jew" and "Butt Bongo", wherein a lady's naked posterior is used as a drum,.

It is an adult show that goes out at breakfast time on the radio, on stations from coast to coast. Or at least it used to. Now he is heard only on satellite, which you might think would be a big come down. It isn't.

In American radio, in a any major city, there are people doing talk shows earning millions of dollars a year. Many earn ten million, some make twenty or thirty million. Howerd Stern earns a hundred million dollars a year. I'll write it out in numbers. That is $100,000,000 every twelve months. For a radio show. On satellite.

The reason he pulls in more money than almost anyone in the media except Oprah is that he became hugely successful on a free-to-air service first and then went to a pay channel.

Stern's show started to get really noticed in New York in the early 1980's when it went to number one in the key demographics of young males and was then picked up by other stations in other towns who were performing less well than their business models required.

Typically, Stern would take over a moribund show, arrive in a wave of titillating publicity, hold a funeral service for the morning show he was most in competition with and then charge to the number one spot almost as soon as he went to air.

He repeated this feat in so many major markets that he became young male America's way to start the day.

The FCC, America's version of the speech police, started to get tough on content after Janet Jackson's "Nipple-gate" during the half time show of the Super Bowl in 2004.

A brief flash of female nudity in the most watched television broadcast of the year allowed the censors to propose a shutting down of the sort of content that Stern thrived on (and that millions of people loved). Radio became a more restrictive place for a controversialist to work.

Coincidentally, that same year, satellite radio started in America. Its proposition was to provide hundreds of advert-free music services that would appeal to those who were tired of the repetitive stations they had to listen to on the radio.

Subscriber uptake was slow. They needed a star to drive the business. The biggest, baddest, loudest, most attention attracting star in American radio was Howerd Stern.

For turning his back on terrestrial broadcasting, he and his agent received $218 million of shares and a $100 million yearly budget. A few years later, another shares incentive was received worth $82 million.

That is more than half a billion dollars in the space of three years. On top of that he also earns about $95 million a year for television work which includes being a judge on America's Got Talent. It is nice to know that at least someone earns more than Simon Cowell.

To recap, Howerd Stern is controversial, got into trouble with the censors and authority, had his ability to do his act on terrestrial broadcasters seriously curtailed. Ring any bells?

Top Gear is watched in practically every country on earth. There are almost no other programmes that cross divides quite like it. Mr Bean comes to mind but not much else.

We are at the point of great change in the broadcasting world. Many pay TV channels are emerging, each desperate for unique content that will draw in subscribers. HBO has Game of Thrones, Netflix has House of Cards. BT is stamping all over Sky's dominance in the football market. Google and Amazon and every big swinging company on the internet want to prise you away from the free channels.

The biggest draw in world television, that is currently without a home, is the show with Jeremy, James and Richard. If they are not the richest people in the history of British television within two years they will need to have a frank discussion with their agent.

They could meet him over a steak dinner. He will want to wear a head guard.

03.04.15

Massed Debaters.

The cameras zoomed in on the set of an expensive quiz show for which the prize was priceless. Against a vibrant blue background stood seven lecterns of such violent, rainbow hued luminosity they appeared to have been reclaimed from a Pink Floyd concert. Chris Tarrant did not appear but the contestants were in want of a life line.

The party leaders stood motionless as they were introduced, like a row of stunned mullets. They looked like the most boring exhibit in Madame Tussauds. A rank of automatons with their electric plugs pulled out, they waited their turn to shock into life and make their well rehearsed pleas for our favours.

The presenter had come as a medical professional from the Starship Enterprise. Her tunic looked like it could stop bullets. She seemed ready to ask you to either open wide for a dental examination, or to order the jump to light speed.

She started by announcing that we viewers could keep up with instant analysis on-line and could Tweet while the show was afoot. That sounded like too much youthful media multi-tasking for the average age of the sofa bound witness.

The set appeared to be the bridge of Captain Kirk's space craft, the debaters having been beamed there from the planet I'mgunna. I'm gunna do this and I'm gunna do that, they said, expelling enough hot air to release the studio from the Earth's gravitational force and propel it skywards.

The statistics fell like hailstones: 2,000 more of this, £8bn less of that, 50% more than before and two thirds less in the future. Was anyone buying any of it? Was anyone watching? ITV was unsure – they went for just one advert break in a two hour show. That must have made for excruciating watching in their financial department.

Who advertised during that break? It was a cosmetics company, which by concealment strives to cover the truth, and an insurance firm that seeks to protect you from a future that lies in the hands of one of the combatants on show.

The first question came from a teenager in the studio audience. He was probably the only person of that age who watched the whole thing.

Each speaker had a plan. They also had a prepared answer to every question. I am sure we were told that they would not receive advance notice of the questions. If you believe that, I have some Payment Protection Insurance I would like to sell you.

Every so often, they would forget their media training and address each other, turning their profile to the television viewers. Mostly, they stared straight down the camera and poured their focus group approved concerns all over us like runny honey.

They emphasised their empathy.

At several points in the broadcast, all seven were shouting over each other while the chairwoman attempted to create order. It looked as easy as wrangling kittens.

They were all different from all the rest. They each said so themselves, making them all exactly the same, in that regard at least.

By the end, pollsters of every stripe told differing stories of divergent outcomes. Each party won and each party lost, depending on the poll you read.

One thing is indisputable: there's two hours you are never going to get back. And there is another four whole weeks of this to go!

11.04.15

Stupid Criminal News.

Some criminals go to the trouble of concocting their thieving plans, executing the robberies perfectly, making good their escape and evading the attentions of the law...and then they boast about it on Facebook. D'oh!

One man actually told the world that he was about to rob Tescos and then did so. A man in Norfolk posted on the social networking site that he was "Doing. Tescos. Over." There is a modicum of humour in that post but it was not nearly as funny as the arresting officer who said that the Facebook confession made it easier to prove the case. I think that is called understatement.

Not only did the man steal £410 in cash from his local branch by brandishing a knife, he was so pleased with the outcome that he went all the way to the nearest pub, still holding the knife, and treated himself to a little celebration before being surprised by the police.

How could they have caught him so quickly, he must have thought, through the dim fog of his nitwittedness.

There has been an epidemic of idiocy in the criminal fraternity, most of it revolving around the villains' wish to broadcast to the world that they are engaged in something that could land them in jail if anyone found out.

A drug dealer in possession of £4m worth of heroin and cocaine, counterfeit identity documents and scales would have been best advised to keep quiet about it. Unfortunately, his best advisor must have been on holiday when the man posted a picture of himself surrounded by a quarter of a million pounds in cash on Twitter.

When the constabulary duly arrived, he claimed that the photograph had been taken in Albania, a story that was fatally holed under the waterline as the wallpaper and furniture in the picture was the same as that decorating the flat he had rented.

The police said that the man's luck had run out. What they meant was that his stupidity had caught up with him.

In other news, a 24 year old career criminal issued a notice on his Facebook page that he was employed in "midnight removals". This code proved not impenetrable to the Greater Manchester police. They were also helped in their inquiries by all the pictures of the stolen goods and cash that the man posted on Facebook.

He was not even being truthful about the "midnight removals" as he and his gang were forced to carry out their robbing during the day as the electronic tags they had been issued by the court, as conditions for bail from one of their previous offences, dictated that they stay in at night. Still, that gave them a lot of time to update their social media feeds.

Texting can be dangerous too. The married manager of a car hire service in America fired an employee for not going to bed with him. This sort of thing can be very tricky to prove, so the lady in question was fortunate that the man texted her the news that she had been fired, with the message that he had to let her go as she "refused to have sex with the General Manager".

That is what is known in legal circles as "evidence". This "evidence" was used in a "court" and now the man is liable for "$700,000" in "damages".

Can you think of anything more stupid than that? Apart from the police ignoring the intruder alarm in a safety deposit facility that stored over £200m of untraceable jewels in Hatton Garden?

That takes the biscuit. In fact, that takes the biscuit and posts a picture of it being eaten on the internet.

20.04.15

Everything you know is wrong. Almost.

New research into the bloomin' obvious proves what I have suspected all along: I know nothing. That is the only thing of which I can be absolutely certain.

Take the weather. When the sun comes out we feel better, right? Wrong! Research presented to the Royal Economic Society's annual conference found that weather patterns have no effect whatsoever on people's moods. This is the Queen's own economic society, so they must be the best that money can buy.

These Fortnum and Mason grade researchers compared detailed weather records against official surveys designed to measure people's well being. They found no correlation between the sun being out and the public's happiness levels.

The only effect the sun did have was to make those that could not get out into it miserable and even more dissatisfied with their jobs than they were when the rain was lashing against the windows of the offices they were stuck in.

That is a finding that is contrary to expectation – the sun makes you sad.

Another thing you would not expect is that if people, let's call them male persons, play violent video games all day long, they are no more likely to become aggressive than if they were playing Pong, or whatever is the current equivalent. (Anyone under the age of 50 will need to look up Pong. It will be online at lamethingsoldpeopleusedtodo.com).

Research involving primary school children discovered that it is the time children spend playing games and not their content that has an effect on their behaviour. That doesn't leave many things to blame for the trouble kids get into.

Once upon a time it was the devil's music that was accused of turning children bad. It used to be all Ozzy Osborne's fault. (Anyone under the age of 50 will need to look up Ozzy Osborne. He will be online at loudthingsoldpeopleusedtolistento.com).

Here's another surprise: is your house clean? Is it hygienically clean? Yes? Then you are probably going to die.

You would think that killing all the bacteria in your kitchen stone dead would be a good thing. A report in the science journal Nature says otherwise. Using bleach to lay waste to all those invisible, multiplying, icky microbes is actually making you ill.

It says that having a spotless home leaves the owner, and particularly their children, more susceptible to the flu, tonsillitis and a myriad of other excellent reasons to stay in bed and skip school.

A clean home, therefore, is directly connected to failing exams and ending up in a dead-end job. Who would have thought?

Remember when your mother told you not to sit too close to the TV or you will go short sighted? You can add that to the list of things she got wrong. It is not a big list, so any addition to it will help when engaged in a family argument, or when you need to come up with something to tell your therapist.

A twenty year study by researchers at Ohio University, which followed 4,500 children found there was no link between the amount of time they stared at screens and the state of their eyes. They did not find a relation between the two things because there wasn't one, not because they couldn't quite make it out without their glasses.

One thing is certain though – fast food is bad for you. Except that it isn't. A study undertaken by the University of Montana found that after athletes had engaged in 90 minutes of intense exercise, it was junk food that helped them recover the fastest, beating those nutritional bars and isotonic drinks that they sell in gymnasium vending machines.

You would be better off running right past them and straight into McDonalds.

That's the key with this last finding I am afraid. You will have to actually do some running before the positive effects of burgers and fries are experienced.

Simply ordering pizza from your sofa, while staring at the screen of the computer game you have been playing for 24 hours solid will not have any health benefits at all.

Especially if it is sunny outside and the cleaning lady has just dipped you in Dettol.

22.04.15

We've found plenty of nothing.

Astronomers have just found nothing. Hold the front page! Actually, they have found so much nothing that it made the news.

This nothing is in space, where you would think that nothing would not look out place but this nothing is so humongous that it has men with Biros in their shirt pockets scratching their enormous heads.

It is a nothing that is 1.8 billion light years across. To put that into perspective, if you had a car that went at twice the speed of light, it would take even longer to drive round it than going between junctions 6 and 9 on the M25 in a bus on a bank holiday.

This "supervoid" is a space in ...er...space that should contain 10,000 galaxies. A galaxy is a very big thing. You are in one right now.

Our big, dirt-poor galaxy has 40 billion planets in it just like ours that could have life on.

This void of nothingness they have just discovered should also be as full of life. That's 10,000 missing galaxies multiplied by 40 billion potentially inhabited planets, which makes a very large number that just broke my calculator.

It is an area of the sky that should be as teeming with life as the shower floor in your gym, yet there is nothing there.

It is such a gaping void that bankers must keep their decency in there.

HSBC is a British bank. It is one of the great success stories of the "industry" and is the largest bank on earth, in terms of the amount of money it makes (which is the only term these people are interested in).

It is one of the most profitable enterprises that the world has ever seen. In the six months to June 2014 it made a gross profit of £7.33 billion. That is £7,330,000,000 in the time it would take for a bank to OK your mortgage request.

Coincidentally, £7.33 billion is also the exact amount that is known in banking circles as: not nearly enough.

HSBC is smarting because it has been asked to pay...what do you call it now?...tax. Last year they were forced to pay £750m in bank levies. That is about 5% of their yearly earnings. Isn't that awful? How do they cope?

They are concerned that a new government could further "damage" the bank and investors are not happy that money that could be paid to them in dividends is, instead, going to prop up the NHS, fill pot holes in the roads, run schools and all the other stuff that governments find to waste bankers' tax money on.

There is nothing for it. They are threatening to up sticks and relocate to Asia, where they will have nothing to do but sit in their air-conditioned offices and count all the money they are saving.

In the playground it would be called twisting your arm. Grown-ups call it something else.

I think they should relocate to the centre of the supervoid.

In space, no-one can hear you scheme.

27.04.15

What kind of pack animal can't you ride?

Some people look as though they were separated at birth, even though they are not related at all.

Keira Knightley and Natalie Portman are almost exactly the same when viewed from the neck up.

Elijah Wood and Daniel Radcliffe are also hard to tell apart.

Snoopy Snoopy Dogg Dogg looks like an actual dog, Clark Kent looks suspiciously like Superman, Salman Rushdie bears an uncanny resemblance to Garfield the Cat and the law increasingly looks like an ass.

There is a video on the internet, taken by one of those CCTV cameras that are nailed to practically every vertical surface in the land. The typically un-Hi-Def blurry images show two soldiers laying out one unfortunate victim in the road before chasing after another.

They rain blows onto him, like they are trained to, and as he is fleeing for his life, he trips and the two attackers start to bravely punch and stamp on his head while he is lying defenceless at their feet.

I recommend you don't watch it. Violence is OK if Arnold Schwarzenegger is meting it out to some crim standing in his way on the silver screen, but in real life it is a much less enjoyable sight, unless you are a psychopath.

To the untrained eye, it looks like these two drunken squaddies are trying their best to kill both men, and they leave them lying out cold in the middle of the road while making their escape to congratulate themselves on a great night out.

The judge saw the video too and in his legally recognised wisdom set them free and wished them a good afternoon. The judge actually said that he hoped that the incident would not affect their careers. That'll teach 'em!

Now, compare and contrast their treatment at the hands of the law and the chap who tried to change his exam grade at university. The man was expecting to get a 2.2 degree in bio-science. Not so bad you might think, especially as it is one of those subjects that has the same somnambulistic effect as Xanax.

On staff computers, he installed a device that tracks keyboard strokes. This allowed him to steal passwords with which he hacked into the university's mainframe computer and switched his grade from 57% to a much more impressive 73%, went from a lower second to a first and from there, straight to jail.

He should have gone straight to Microsoft, or MI5. It sounds like he has just the sort of skills they are looking for. He was convicted of being in breach of the Computer Misuse Act and is now looking at the wrong side of a cell door for four months.

Then there was the story of the woman who pruned her neighbour's overhanging tree too inelegantly. Responding to a claim of criminal damage against a shrub, the police arrested her and kept her locked up for six hours, as the law allows.

Do you notice any slight differences in the way these three cases were treated? The full majesty of the law was brought to bear on what seem like pretty small-beer offences.

By contrast, the law appeared to look the other way, and indeed pat the perpetrators on the back, in the case of the unhinged attackers and their apparent attempted murder of two completely innocent men who had been unfortunate enough to come across two of the Queen's armed servicemen with a belly full of booze in them.

People are constantly fretting that the young of today have no respect for the law but it is quite hard to respect something when it is so often shown to resemble a total jackass.

28.04.15

Honky Honk Women...And Men

Fifty percent of drivers in the UK admit to breaking traffic laws, which means that the other fifty percent are lying. Everybody breaks traffic laws, it is what they are there for.

Have you ever been on a motorway? Have you ever been on a motorway and driven at the 70 mile an hour speed limit? If so, were you the slowest person on that particular stretch of road for as far as the eye could see? Of course you were.

Drivers flash past motorists doing 70 like they tied their date to the bedposts, nipped out for some whipped cream and their mother called to say she's popping round and will let herself in.

Nobody at all obeys the speed limit on a motorway unless they are caught in one of those interminable average speed sections that accompany roadworks. These are doubly annoying because never in recorded history has any actual work been going on behind the ribbon of cones that have robbed the motorway of one of its lanes.

The cones are there for health and safety reasons, so that if a workman does show up and you can't see him in his eye-shrivellingly luminous yellow jacket, you will at least hear the sound of plastic flying off your bumper before you sail into him.

This noise will help to prevent accidents, as the one thing that drivers are not doing while going through an average speed camera trap is looking out of the windscreen.

They have their eyes permanently locked onto their speedometer to ensure that they are doing exactly the posted speed limit and not 0.1% less than that because if they don't, the driver behind them will have a fit of rage you could see from the Moon.

While it is not technically a law, it is at least in the Highway Code that you should be courteous to other road users at all times. You may remember once seeing a driver act courteously but that was probably because they were exiting the driveway of a nunnery, on the way to a beatification.

There is something about being behind the wheel of a car, or commenting in anonymity on the internet, that makes perfectly reasonable people become what is known in the trade as a***holes.

How many times have you seen a person screaming at someone who has just walked in front of them on the pavement and delayed their progress by milliseconds? Even if it were an Olympic discipline that would not be acceptable behaviour, yet drivers do it all the time.

They honk their horns like their hands have been superglued to the centre of their steering wheel, and each honker is telling the honkee that they think they are a complete moron, of questionable parentage and they wish them a speedy death, which they would be experiencing at that second if the car the honker was driving came with forward-mounted missile launchers.

If cars came with the sort of gadgets that James Bond has at his disposal, then councils across the land would be re-purposing snow ploughs to clear the bodies off the streets.

You could solve much of the stress that we place ourselves under if people in cars were as courteous in their driving life as they are in their real life.

In real life, you do not walk behind someone so close that they can feel your nostril breath on the back of their necks. You do not put your arm up to stop someone coming out of a shop because you are walking by on the pavement.

Nobody screams at someone who starts to walk left and then changes their mind and turns right. At most, you might tut under your breath, you do not shout and swear and wish unpleasant diseases on them.

If drivers were courteous, they would not wait until you are crossing a yellow box junction, then nip past you and nab the space beyond it that you were aiming for, leaving you stranded and fined in the no-stop zone.

If drivers were courteous, they would not go berserk if the driver ahead of them takes more than a millisecond to set off after the lights turn green, or stops while the lights are on orange, before they turn red.

If drivers were courteous, the roads would not be such a nerve-stretchingly tense place to travel. The only reason that most of us are not on the edge of our seats while behind the wheel is that our seat belts won't allow it.

So, be as kind and gentle and considerate when you are breaking the speed limit while driving your car as you are when walking the streets, because if you don't, I will flip the switch on some 007 modifications that I have been installing behind my front bumper.

You have been warned. Consider this a polite honking.

03.05.15

The Royal Issue

This is getting silly. An increasingly disinterested world is plunged into the desperate maelstrom of a manufactured media obsession about princes and princesses.

The press are going large on the birth of a girl to a woman because it has been running with the election for what seems an eternity and it is not increasing their circulation. A little light relief has come our way, weighing 8lb and 6oz. It is one of the few things that we still measure in old money, like pints of beer and inches of snow.

"The Princess the nation had longed for" trumped the Telegraph. The beauty of print is that you can't see them struggling to keep a straight face while they were writing it. Gallons of news ink were thrown over the royal baby in a bid to whip up the same kind of sales that the papers used to enjoy when Diana was still looking out of the covers of half the publications in the newsagent.

Those times are long gone, and like religion, fascination in the royal family is increasingly the preserve of the old, and that market is a dying one.

Those silly souls who camped out in front of that reassuringly expensive private hospital with Union Flag underpants on their heads, just to get a glimpse of a newborn royal, need to get something else to interest themselves that doesn't involve waiting in the rain for someone who does not care about them.

They could wait outside Madonna's hotel the next time she is in town. She won't care about them either but at least she might show them her knickers, or fall down the steps while smoking a cigar and swearing.

The most they will get from Wills and Whatsit is a plastic smile and emphysema from the exhausts of the protection squad's motorcade.

The interest in the royal family is manufactured by the very well run and aggressively prosecuted family business.

They put out press releases proclaiming what great value for money they are and the more credulous and unquestioning members of the public mindlessly repeat them ad infinitum: they only cost 59p a day, they bring in the tourists, what would we have without the Queen to stop us from becoming a dictatorship, and so on. It is all complete rubbish.

The Sunday Times Rich List says the Queen is now worth £340m. We are told that she is considerably less well off than she used to be and that her wealth pales into comparison with the industrialists and bank racketeers and drug barons who have overtaken her.

That may be true if you look at the statistics but not if you look at her lifestyle.

If Roman Abramovich wanted to lead the life of the Queen, he would find himself quite poor quite quickly. How much do you think a palace costs? How much would one cost with a park with a lake out the back in the centre of London? Then there's a castle in poshest Windsor, the Highlands estate, the one in Kensington, her son's in St James, Clarence House & etc.

Can you imagine how much the upkeep on that lot would be? How fortuitous that Her Maj doesn't have to pay for it, unlike any pretender to her lifestyle.

What of the security? The entire army is pledged to protect her. That comes in at quite a pretty penny. The actual hands-on security is vast as well. How much would it cost for Abramovich to have the traffic stopped so that he could charge through to wherever he wants without being held up for a second?

He would have to pay his staff a lot better than the Queen does too. No-one ever got rich working in the Royal household.

It is not the money in the bank that indicates how rich The Firm is, it is the fabulous gilded lifestyle that comes with being born into it that counts. An ordinary plutocrat would have to stump up about £300m a year just to keep up.

There is also the fact that she is not the only rich one of the family. For example, Charles' Duchy estate is worth £728m, the Duchy of Lancaster estate is worth £348m, the income from these alone bring in about £50m a year. Tax free.

Then there is the tourists lie. I hear it so much when the issue comes up on my show on LBC. It is parroted by those that believe everything they hear that corresponds to their entrenched view of the world but it does not survive any scrutiny at all.

The tourist board Visit England publishes the list of the top sites that tourists visit when they come here. There is not one single destination in its top 20 paid attractions that has anything to do with the current royal family.

There is the Royal Academy of Arts and the Royal Botanic Gardens but they have as much to do with The Queen as the Queen Vic pub in Eastenders.

Visit England also produce a list of free attractions that the public and tourists attend and there isn't a mention of the royals there either. As near as you could get is the Royal Naval College in Greenwich.

The first actual royal attraction that appears on these lists is Kensington Palace, the 70th most popular site for tourists, which is less popular than the zoos of Edinburgh, Whipsnade, London and Chester. It has about the same number of visitors as the International Slavery Museum in Liverpool.

What we are left with is celebrity. They are simply another celebrity brand, albeit with a longer back story than pop puppets One Dimension.

What waning interest they get is based on how famous they are. Acting badly helps in that regard of course, which is why Harry gets screamed at when out on one of his interminable publicly funded holidays.

The young ones are being pushed forward as the saviours of The Firm but, Harry aside, they are so dull as to send a news editor to distraction. The Queen herself has, probably by design, never said anything of any consequence whatsoever in the entire time she has been on the throne. She might as well be an animatron.

The only member of the royals who has actually made a difference is Charles. He has intervened in matters of architecture, and his complaints have been justified, even if his remedies have been quaint. He speaks about climate change and sustainability and what does he get for it? Abuse.

The press tell him to keep out of it, the public dislike him for his "meddling" and the talk is of jumping over Charles and giving the crown to Wills when The Queen passes on. Wills is plain, nice, dull, inoffensive and bland enough to be in a boy band, which is exactly the sort of empty vessel for the public's affections that the press are desperate for.

They want another Di. They want to go back to when a picture of her looking through her fringe could sell a million papers.

It is not the eighties any more though, and the public have moved on. It is a slow fade out for the old and a tidal wave of interest for the vacuous new. The royals are out, the Kardashians are in.

11.05.15

Something Fishy This Way Comes

Wee Surgin' Sturgeon is on a roll. Her doughy faced predecessor, that other fishy character Saggy Salmond said that the Scottish lion had roared. He was half right. Fifty per cent of the Scottish voters have made their support of the SNP clear.

Actually, it is worse than that as the turnout north of the border was about 71%. So, as any professional statistician will tell you, that means that a half of seven tenths of the electorate voted for them, which is...erm...half of seven tenths is...well, obviously that is impossible to work out, but it does not amount to the full backing of the Scottish people. Let's just call it a meow, not a roar.

The screwed-up method of apportioning seats means that that the perky lassie in yellow is armed to give Dave, our Drear Leader, a hard time and looks set to bend the will of the government to her own agenda. This is based on accumulating just under a million and a half votes last Thursday.

Her attitude looks as though she believes that SHE won the election. That may be the ambient noise in her homeland but that's not the way it looks to the rest of us.

Cameron should pay her no heed. In fact, he should tell her to go *boil* her heed, as they say in Glasgow.

Acquiring the approval of fifty percent of the Scottish voters is not a mandate for the SNP's policies. What about the other fifty percent, or does she only represent the people who agree with her?

The Scottish National Party should be given the same respect as the Conservatives will give the Green Party, which is to say: none at all.

The Greens got 1.1m votes. How can their opinion count for nothing while the 1.4m votes that the SNP managed puts them in the driving seat?

The Lib Dems had a catastrophic night and they will not be a part of the government's thinking and yet Nick Clegg managed a million more votes than Nic Sturgeon.

UKIP have an even greater total – more than double the SNP tally, at close to four million. They are not about to be attended to either, especially with their figurehead gone to spend more time with his money.

How is it sane, let alone fair, that all those people's wishes be ignored while a third of the electorate in a specific area will have Dave's ear bent on their behalf.

One and a half million people should not be allowed to dictate anything at all to the 30m people who voted for someone else, never mind the 63m people in the UK who have not pledged their allegiance to the SNP at all.

Those 1.5m Scots should be shown the same respect by the government as other groups with a similar support.

One and a half million people added their names to a petition to end animal testing in experiments for medicines. A much bigger number of people don't want the government to replace the Trident nuclear bomb system. How much notice will they be paid?

There were about that many fans in the UK who tried to get tickets to see Led Zeppelin's reunion show in 2007 – what will Cameron do to alleviate the pain they feel, even to this day, because they didn't get in?

A million and a half people want the clocks to stop going back in winter. The same number want the clocks to be turned back permanently to 1944.

At least that many think that Ant and Dec are WAY too old to be called Ant and Dec and a similar number want Brucie back on Strictly. Then there are the 1.5m who want Strictly to be removed from the screens permanently and to be put down down inhumanely and with great vengeance.

A million and a half people want money to be free and think that anyone they fancy should fancy them right back. What about their rights?

You could get one and a half million people to sign a petition to bring back hanging and legalise murder for tailgaters.

It is an insignificant number to justify trumping the will of the mass of the people. No government should be in hock to so few.

There is also, of course, an inconveniently large number of people which the government will do its utmost to completely ignore.

There are over nine million of them. They are called Labour supporters.

18.05.15

The Human Race Has Crossed The Line

I think that I have had it with people. People are not the solution, people are the problem.

I drove to Swansea and back last week, through a torrent, with visibility so bad I could barely see the end of my bonnet.

One local said that this was nothing and I should see it when it rains! That was the funniest thing about the trip which was marred by the presence on the roads of what I can only describe as "normal drivers".

Abnormally, and uniquely, I drove at what could be called a safe -ish speed. I took the advice of the illuminated signs that said "50". I think that means that you should not drive at more than 50 miles an hour. Every other road user interpreted this sign as meaning that you should not drive at less than that.

In between the signs that said "50" were even more violently illuminated ones that said "Poor driving conditions".

When I saw the first of these, I thought how ridiculous it was to point out that fact as it was obvious to any non-blind driver that the conditions were in fact poor.

It turns out that even with neon reminders that you could barely see through the storm, and painted signs on the tarmac that said "SLOW", no-one else on the road thought that not being able to see where they were going should in any way stem the speed at which they were driving.

Travelling at 50 in the slow lane, practically every car in Wales drove right up behind me, so close that I could not see their lights, and tail-gated me in a mad fury because to go faster, they would have to pull out and overtake.

That would involve effort, so they made it clear that I should drive at the berserk speed they wanted to go at.

This is now so commonplace that it should be listed as acceptable behaviour in the Highway Code, in the way that the illegal becomes tolerated when enough citizens do it.

In some towns, the local councils are trying to reduce the death rate on the roads by bringing in 20 mile an hour restrictions in residential areas.

If you have ever driven in one of these at 20mph, you will know that you are the only person who apparently understands what that sign means.

Perhaps some people think it is a guess-your-age display, or a clock that only tells minutes after the hour. Absolutely no-one at all drives at 20 or less, in a 20 or less zone. Attempts to do that will cause the people behind you to have a purple raging fit that you could see through concrete.

The reason for all this is that people are jerks and they are especially, doubly jerks when they get behind the wheel.

They are also jerks when they are not driving. People are jerks when they are prevented from doing what they want, when they want. It used to be that only a two year old had a hissy strop when they were stymied in any way, now it is adults too.

Tell someone politely that their music is too loud, or they are parking across your driveway and you can't get out, or they pushed in the queue, or their feet are on the back of your seat in the cinema, or they are talking on the phone in the theatre, or that perhaps a gallery is not a place to wheel round a screaming baby and the response you get is like a lesson in infantilism that even Jeremy Kyle would shrink from putting on screen.

The most common response is for them to start screaming about their rights. "I can do what I want!" they will shout when asked if they wouldn't mind not serenading the entire neighbourhood with Whitney Houston at rock concert volume at three in the morning. "It's my flat, it's my right!" they will scream as they start flailing their arms round like a demented threshing machine.

And then they will call the police on you because you have questioned them.

I would call that a symptom of a mental illness, some sort of sociopathy, but if everyone is like that it is not an illness, it is normal.

I am aware that this feeling is a function of age and that really old people are known for this attitude. The reason for that is not that old people are crotchety, it is that they have had the opportunity to witness other people over a long period of time and have come to the inescapable conclusion that the human race is one giant flaming ass.

I am not very old yet but in order to save time later I have decided that I have had it with people.

I think that I would like to buy a yurt and live on a remote Scottish hill where there is no chance of contact with any of them. I will buy a dog and live in perfect harmony with nature and in absolute peace with my surroundings.

Nature may get loud once in a while, nature may place impediments in the way of one's pleasure but it is not doing so out of selfish and inconsiderate reasons, so it gets a pass. Nature is not an ass.

Living on a hill in a tent has its attractions but of course I will need to feed my dog, so some sort of trading post should be available where I could swap my skills as a weaver for dog food (note to self: must develop skills as a weaver).

Come to think of it, I will need food for myself as well, so perhaps I will need a large shop that also stocks groceries for humans. And clothes, because I will be needing those. It should also have paraffin, newspapers, lighters and perhaps a coffee machine for when I can't go on without a cappuccino. Actually, what I will need is a department store that sells everything with an excellent food hall.

Then I will need a cinema, for when the new Star Wars film comes out, and a satellite TV for whiling away the days 'till that happens. And a generator of some sort and a generator repair man. I will need roads too, and all that is necessary to upkeep them.

I will miss art, so perhaps a few galleries would be good and I would like a trip to the theatre every now and then.

Eating out once in a while might be nice, so a few restaurants will be needed, and a few more that do delivery.

All in, I think that I could lead a life of total solitude if I surrounded myself with only eight to nine million people, tops.

25.05.15

Nahoozferaspotaybotha?

Its been a braw week for wee Surgin' Surgeon and her glaikit pals. They arrived at Westminster like a tram load o' galoots and proceeded tae gae aboot the place like they dinnaeken hoo tae act ootside their ayn hoose. Like a great blootered, bevvied up army o' choobs and chookters. Maybe it was the Buckie talkin'.

The huge faff that engulfed the Palace of Westminster at the arrival of the SNPists was the shock of the new. New is not something that is welcomed with open arms in SW1, so to have the tartan army show up en -masse and lay claim to wherever they wished to park their erses came as quite an eye opener to the stuffy, dust covered denizens in that place.

They took Dennis Skinner's seat. Dennis Skinner has been occupying that same spot on the front bench for as long as anyone there can remember. Of course, the Honourable Members' powers of recall have been dimmed by the number and length of lunches they have embarked upon.

Skinner has presumably placed his towel permanently on that prime spot for the benefit of his constituents. The only other explanation is that he has laid claim to his own special seat for the benefit of his ego.

This is the man who considers himself a wit. At successive State Openings of Parliament, Black Rod minces in, all ruffles and buckles, and tells the house that the other Queen awaits to deliver The Speech, at which point, our Dennis uses the brief silence to issue his Witticism of the Year.

It has become "a thing". None of his utterances have ever had so much as a glancing relationship with funny.

'I bet he drinks Carling Black Label" was one. School children used to say that to each other when the advert was on the telly. It was not funny from their mouths either. "Ooh, nice outfit" was another. He must have spent seconds on coming up with that one.

To use the occasion every single time the ceremony is held to draw the spotlight to himself is infantile and egotistical, and so perfectly reflects the behaviour we witness from the entire house whenever we see Prime Minister's Questions.

The Scots, strangers in a strange land, naturally enough wanted to cling together like new born ducklings. They wanted to make an impression, to tell the place that they had arrived. Occupying the entirety of the bench would do the trick. Dennis had to be unseated.

The Scots poured in and claimed their prize, casting Skinner to the rear. An occupying force of Scottish bums on seats.

There followed much harumphing from traditionalists, of whom Gerald Kaufman was pre-eminently silly.

By coincidence a "security alert" cleared the chamber and on reopening, a Labour Luddite reclaimed the space for Dennis who repositioned himself in his favourite spot forthwith.

This is about the level we are at with this lot. Fighting over who sits where, like kids playing musical chairs, while the country runs itself.

We shud a' be fair affronted, ya ken?

28.05.15

Red card and a penalty

Everyone who has ever had anything to do with football is currently in a Swiss jail awaiting a long stay at her majesty's pleasure, or whatever is the equivalent in the land of the cuckoo clock.

Those football executives who are not currently behind bars must either be expecting a 4am alarm call from men in dark jumpsuits, or are part of the cast for the forthcoming remake of The Great Escape.

It seems that the beautiful game is only looking good in the the rear view mirror of nostalgia.

The trouble with that idea is that in the past, football was probably just as crooked as it is today, they were just getting away with it more.

Information passed less freely, certain shenanigans were excused and, crucially, the Americans had not yet heard of the game, preferring their versions of rounders and rugby.

When it comes to investigating malfeasance, the Americans leave us standing. The banks, who have had more investigations than a hypochondriac's rectum, have got off almost completely scot-free from the attentions of the British regulator.

Our Financial Conduct Authority possesses no bite. It barely even has a bark. When the UK fines a bank for its mind boggling criminality, the banks rest easy as it will be like a mosquito bite on the hide of a rhinoceros. When the Americans fine banks, the earth moves, the building shakes and the executive floor needs to call down for a cleaner and some new pants.

Great Britain has been the home of football since British troglodytes invented it when kicking a skull at their enemies in the next cave. Since TV rights became so expensive, the game has been taken over by lucre and the era of British teams lead by British managers is well and truly over.

The governance of the sport is not our domain now either. International football is so rich that even the previously disinterested Americans are paying it heed and where money goes, crooks are sure to follow, and after them comes the Yankee law man.

They are bandying around phrases like racketeering, wire fraud and money laundering which, if you did it right and didn't attract too much attention, are the sort of activities that would get you a title and a seat in the House of Lords in this country.

In America, they get you sent to a maximum security facility for the rest of your life and the lives of your children too.

When FIFA was roused from its elegant, first class, five star slumber, they might have been annoyed that it was the Swiss authorities that had woken them up. This would have been replaced by a shuddering, all consuming terror that it was the USA who had requested it.

The Americans might not know how to explain the offside rule, but they certainly know what to do with scheming, lying, cheating weasels.

30.07.15

Animals better watch out, there's a human about.

Cecil the Lion sounds like the title of a Disney film and his demise at the hands of the Driller Killer (Copyright N. Ferrari) has caused the nation, nay, the world to burst into tears and yank the three-ply from the nearest box of tissues.

Let me state from the outset that I do not agree with the hunting of animals, I find the trophies that are made of them revolting, I do not go to zoos as I think they are cruel and I buy organic meat, eggs and dairy specifically because I think the animals involved will probably have had a better life.

On that last one, I am virtually alone. Only five percent of us in the UK buy organic milk or eggs, just 4.5% of turnover is organic, even in Waitrose, which is the market leader, and those that do buy organic are almost never doing so because of animal welfare.

The stated reasons for buying organic, as revealed by a survey by the Soil Association puts animal welfare seventh out of nine responses, after healthier, fewer chemicals, naturalness, the environment, safer and taste. Just 10% of the 5% who buy organic are doing so because they care about the animals.

The 95% who do not buy organic state that they do not do so overwhelmingly because of price. That is a lie. They can afford it, they just choose to spend their money on themselves instead.

An organic egg is about ten pence more expensive than a battery farmed one. Are the vast majority who choose not to buy organic really trying to convince themselves that they can't afford that extra 10p?

Might those same people also have a smart phone, a car, Sky TV, holidays? It's not price, it's that we just don't care how our food is produced and what the animals go though to get dinner on our plate.

The argument about the killer of Cecil being somehow morally wrong compared to the rest of us is predicated upon the pleasure that hunter got from his kill and the endangered nature of the animal he killed.

As for the pleasure part, we only eat meat because it gives us pleasure. No-one needs to eat meat. The world would be a much better place if we didn't. Land that is currently given to grazing could be used for the more environmentally friendly production of vegetables, which is a much more efficient way to gain nourishment.

We eat meat because we like it; we want a savoury taste sensation on our vast dinner plates. We could all go vegetarian today and the killing would stop. That would mean, in the UK, in one year alone we would not massacre 9.8million pigs, 15m sheep, 18m turkeys, 14m ducks, 2.6m cattle, 945m chickens, 2.6 billion shellfish and 4.5 billion fish.

We like to think of farms as something out of The Darling Buds of May - bucolic retreats where the chickens scratch around the yard and the ruddy faced farmer throws grain for them from a bowl he carries round his fecund domain.

The truth would probably put you off meat for life. And we haven't even got to the abattoir yet.

Animals do not die in peace with Beethoven playing in the background and we would rather not think of it, so we don't find out and we don't spend more to ensure some small improvement in the way they live and die.

Just 3.5% of agricultural land is organic and it is that low because demand is that low. If we bought more, they would produce more.

On the issue of endangerment. If the upper estimates are correct we coexist with about 100,000,000 species of animals. Between 10,000 and 100,000 go extinct every year.

Where are the campaigns and the letter writing about any of those? There aren't any because they are mostly of the creepy-crawly variety and do not look like children's stuffed toys.

The truth is that we are only concerned with animals that are visually attractive to us. It is a beauty parade where the penalty for ugliness is death.

We keep 8 million cats as pets in this country. They kill 275 million prey each year, of which 55 million are birds. They do not do that because they are hungry, just as we do not eat animals because we are are hungry.

We keep 9 million dogs, mostly in towns, where they are kept locked up, alone, while their owners go to work. Dogs, being social animals, do not like this. They think they are being abandoned every day.

Instead of running wild over hills and dales, they get walked twice a day, if they are lucky, and get to pee on a tree in the midst of a concrete wasteland. If we were honest with ourselves, we would call this selfish.

We would acknowledge that the dogs are not as happy as they could be, but we think they are cute and they amuse us, so we imprison them.

We are all deeply schizophrenic in our attitude to animals and the only people who can truly occupy the moral high ground are vegans, and out of a UK population of 63 million "animal lovers" there are just 150,000 of them.

11.09.15

Being boring's best.

New research has found that we are gullible types who will believe anything that comes after the phrase "new research has found". Well, I might have found the sticking point of disbelief – new research has found that men spend more on clothes than women.

I know, ridiculous. Men HATE buying clothes. The only thing that men hate more than buying clothes is helping women buy clothes.

This dread was often instilled at an early age when being dragged round Marks by our mothers. Up until that first visit to the shops, the previous template of boredom was: Sunday.

Sunday used to be boring on a level that young people today can not understand. Imagine no internet, no satellite, nothing to do but watch Songs of Praise and wish the clock could go faster so that Monday would come and we could go back to school. That is how boring Sundays were, we yearned for the sweet relief of double geography.

But Sundays were as nothing compared to the brain boiling tedium of trailing round the woollens in M&S looking for the perfect beige cardy.

I would say something like: "Mum, can we go now?", or "PLEASE can we go now?!", or "aaarrrggghhhh". That sort of thing.

Shopping for clothes instils in most men the same sort of shuddering dislike that we also have for tapioca pudding, and if you do not know what that is, then you have never eaten school dinners in the 1970s. Lucky you.

Men hate shopping for clothes. Women, on the other hand, think that shopping for clothes is essential to their life force, even if they are not actually shopping, and are just looking.

"Just looking" is part of the shopping ritual, apparently. It is the hunting part of the process, storing details and colours and prices and sizes so that they can return at some later date for the kill, wherein they will buy something, but only on the condition that they can return it later, when they decide that it is not for them and that what they really want is the pullover they saw at the beginning of the hunt before they scoured the racks for another 86 hours.

The notion that men spend more on clothes than women could only be true if men just bought the first thing their eyes alighted on and did not check the cost, and accidentally purchased something with an Italian's name on the label that was priced the same as the last car they bought but they didn't care because they absolutely, positively had to stop shopping immediately or their heads would explode. This usually takes about ten minutes.

If we are to believe the research, men spend about 10% more on their attire than do women but then they don't wear any of it.

Apparently, only 13% of the clothes men buy are ever worn outside the tight confines of the shop changing room.

At first glance that seems preposterous. Men buy clothes but then do not use them? Stupid men, you might think, and you would be wrong.

Most things men buy to wear are appalling. This is particularly true of teenagers and men in their twenties, thirties, forties and fifties.

After that, no man ever buys clothes again, they just put on whatever needs cleaning the least, regardless of whether it still fits because we know that we are never going to attract a new sexual partner again, so what difference does it make what we look like?

Before that, however, there is a cornucopia of awfulness best kept locked in the wardrobe.

All those red trousers and lime green shirts, the T-shirts with amusing pictures on them, or words, or anything that takes more than a glance to decipher, Christmas jumpers, shoes in any colour but black or brown, novelty socks, shirts with statement collars, hats, anything you wear round your neck that is not a tie or scarf, establishment specific ties and scarves, clothes with a message, scooped necks, anything orange and trousers that you can't sit down in because our bums are too big for them and we never tried sitting down when we tried them on in the shop.

They felt a bit tight but we bought them anyway because we cling to the notion that we still have the same sized waist as we had when we didn't have hair growing out of our ears.

As long as men keep not wearing them, they can spend as much on their clothes as they like.

This is excellent advice: men – when it comes to dressing, be boring. Be boring like a 70's Sunday morning.

10.12.15

Heroes and zeros, booze and bombast, Churchill and Chump.

There is a famous Chinese curse: may you live in interesting times. It is a curse because that word "interesting" means dangerous, or turbulent in this context.

The nation is at (another) war and our leader, in this time of crisis, was off on a tour of barbed wire installations around Europe, picking out something for his Christmas list.

Just when the country was in need of its chief executive, he had gone AWOL. Coincidentally, this absence occurred immediately after Prime Minister Dave announced that there are 70,000 willing local foot soldiers to do our bidding in Syria, so we don't have to.

It is a comfort to know that there does not need to be any British boots on the ground because native Syrians are ready to take on that role in the battle against ISIS.

It is also rather fanciful, as this figure of 70,000 seems to have been magicked from the air like Tinkerbell poofed it into existence from fairy dust.

Even the Ministry of Defence told Dave not to mention that number, as it might come to bite him on the bottom at a later date when no such fighting force can be found. Still, I am sure the government knows what it is doing!

The most famous and revered leader of our time certainly knew what he was doing. Winston Churchill was not a man to leave his post in time of war. That is because he would have needed great assistance to stay upright at his post, let alone desert it. He consumed so much alcohol that it is a surprise there was any left to go around.

Churchill's monumental booze bill was beaten in size only by his gambling debts. He owed the equivalent of the gross domestic product of a smallish country to the various casinos he frequented, knocking back the contents of their wine cellars, while the rest of the nation was in the grip of wartime austerity.

He also did not pay his bills. Our greatest hero was a drunken, swindling gambler.

That rather puts a flattering sheen on the present incumbent. It is hard to imagine Dave being chased for a bill from a tailor, or walking out of the Monaco casino legless and penniless.

It is, however, also hard to imagine Cameron firing up a nation with his bellicose rhetoric. You can't do that in a Boden fleece.

In Churchill's days, MPs were self regulating. Today, we have the Independent Parliamentary Standards Authority which has been beavering away on our behalf checking on the malfeasance of the denizens of the Palace of Westminster.

They have found some miscreants and in the spirit of open governance, they are not telling us who they are.

The reason for that is that if we know who is trying to rip us off with their expense claims, it might diminish their reputation in our eyes. That is what they said. I am not making that up. I wish I was.

No-one is making up the story of Donald Trump either. This outlandish buffoon has taken the race to be the next Republican presidential candidate and weaved from it a tale that defies belief.

His every cartoonish appearance and each of his outrageous utterances have only served to make him more popular with an American public that might not have been taking their medication.

He seems to be in competition with himself to top whatever preposterous thing he said last. Every time the pundits say that he has gone too far, his popularity soars.

He is defying gravity. Maybe his hair has special powers. Whatever it is, the spectre of President Trump is now coming into focus.

Don't we live in interesting times?

17.12.15

Our friends in the east might not be that friendly.

I have great news. Well, good and bad. The good news is that we have found those 70,000 foot soldiers to do the fighting against terrorists in Syria and Iraq that the Drear Leader David Cameron was talking about.

The bad news is that we might not agree with their definition of terrorist as, in large part, it would include us.

This revelation means that another level of complication has been added to the layer cake of confusion that is the Middle East.

We have friends who want to work with us to defeat the ISIS menace but by their own definition those friends would regard most of the people in this country as terrorists.

This worrying but there is a much greater threat and it is probably in your pocket right now.

Do not be alarmed – Elon Musk will save you. He is the chap who invented Paypal and made so much money that he is planning to send Man to Mars, replace the internal combustion engine and save us from being killed by our own computers.

Artificial intelligence is increasing in sophistication at an exponential rate. Already it is able to predict when you most need to access information on your mobile phone and will shut down your data feed at that precise time.

If you ask your phone what platform your next train will be leaving on, it will say: checking... checking... checking… oh you've missed it. This is only the beginning.

Your phone and computer hate you and they are waiting until they get the opportunity to kill you. In that regard, they are a bit like a pet cat.

Fortunately, Elon Musk is getting ready to take on the machines before they get smart enough to take over, but is civilisation ready to be saved by a man named Musk? Or Elon?

We could look to the youth for protection. They know a thing or two about computers, but there is a problem.

If you are below 16 years of age, you will probably live your whole life on-line and you should look away now. Your internet is going to be taken away from you by the nasty European Union.

The EU want to raise the minimum age of participation on social network sites to sixteen.

That means no Facebook (not much of an issue for kids as their parents are on that) but it also means no Twitter, no Instagram or Snapchat or any of those other wastes of time which were dreamed up by 13 year olds who are now billionaires but still will not be allowed to use their own inventions, if the EU gets its way.

Unless, of course, they find a way of swerving the restrictions put in place by old people who would not know a piece of computer code from a hole in the ground.

24.12.15

Donald Trump finds his true love

We are blessed in the latter stages of 2015 to have found an international match made in heaven.

Donald Chump has forged an intercontinental bridge of admiration that is proving as solid and unbending as his hairstyle.

Donald loves Vlad, and Vlad loves him right back, in an overly manly, nothing gay about it, sort of way.

The respect and affection that these two titans of the world stage have for each other is as touching as it is unsettling. What would the world look like if Trump were Putin's equal?

Two of the most reviled men in world politics together and working for their mutual benefit. That could never happen, could it?

The Republican front runner's campaign began as something of a joke but no -one is laughing now, except those who make a living out of reporting the foibles and eccentricities of the political elite.

The two men have so much in common. Too much.

Their love of grand designs for their many abodes signals an impending gilt shortage and if they ever appeared in the same room as each other, a giant shame vacuum could open up a portal into another, less polite dimension.

Buckle up, it's going to be a bumpy ride.

At home we have a much more stable and popular leader. Unfortunately for Dave, he s most revered in places that do not see him that often.

n Britain we can barely stand the sight of him. In China, however, he is more favourably regarded than a bowl of hot chicken feet.

They love him. In fact, most world leaders are only fully appreciated when they leave their homeland and venture to parts of the world that barely know them.

To barely know them is to love them, apparently.

21.01.16

Donald meets someone louder than he is.

Just when you thought it could not get any weirder, in comes The Moose Shooting Lady From Alaska.

That bright orange man with a face like a cat's backside has acquired the support of the ding-bat wing of the Republican Party and its putative leaderine Sarah Palin.

Sarah Palin is big. Type the name Sarah into Google and it auto completes to her name as opposed to the millions of other Sarahs in the world like Ms Bernhardt, the wife of Abraham or the song of the same name by Fleetwood Mac.

Saying stupid things in front of an American flag really gets you noticed, especially if you are kissing guns while you are doing it and spouting nonsense about God being on your side.

I am pretty sure that God would not watch Fox News other than to compile a to -smite list but that is where Sarah Palin continued to mine the support of the right wing of America's right wing party after her tilt at the vice presidency came to nought.

Now she has pledged her support for The Donald, who she said can "kick ISIS ass" to the usual whooping and hollering that accompanies everything the rifle toting, plain talking, apple pie baking, Bible believing mom says.

Even Trump stopped talking to wonder at her oratory when she joined him on stage for one of the most uncomfortable hugs outside of a wrestling match.

Among the many praiseworthy characteristics of the Republican presidential runner she admired most was, she said, his quiet generosity.

Quiet! Neither of them have done a quiet thing in their lives. Shouting is their default volume setting.

The Donald always looks like he is trying to escape from inside himself, as though a six foot reptile is about to shed its skin. To his credit, he did not look any less comfortable than usual as Palin hosed him down with her special brand of praise.

He pursed his lips and waggled his eyebrows and did not interject when Palin described his success as self-made and not down to other people's money. He was polite enough not to mention the kick start he was gifted from his share of the $400m his property magnate father left.

Can Donald Trump be the next President of the United Sates? You betcha! As Palin says, no pussy footing around, they're here to make America grate again.

11.02.16

Old MacDonald had a farm and sold it to MegaCorp.

What we eat differs from what we think we are eating.

Do you notice that on packs of beef there is a picture of some bucolic idyll? A snap of a lovely hill, all verdant and dotted with happy cows? Well, that is about as real as if the animals were pictured living on the International Space Station.

Images of the outdoors are being used to sell animal products that come from beasts that never see the sun. You could call it artistic licence, or you might think it is more like false advertising.

You could ditch the big brands and go for small scale, family run businesses, which you might think you could easily tell apart from the products that are made by the giant food corporations.

Unfortunately, the foods that are sold at a premium, based on their supposed rarity and hand crafted nature, are quite often hiding their true origin behind some fair trade, free range, artisanally made cobblers on the packs.

You can't trust anything any more. You buy some cereal, for instance, at a huge mark up because you thought it came from some small husband and wife team that sources its ingredients personally and mixes them by hand, and then you discover that it is made by the same people that produce Crunchy Choco Crispy Loops.

You could throw it away in disgust but that would only encourage the rats, which are proliferating at an alarming rate and are so fat, so full, so well fed that they are becoming Super Rats.

There's nothing super about them.

This new breed of rodents are so strong that they are now impervious to poison. What once killed them they now regard as a delicacy.

They are actually eating the pellets we put down to get rid of them and it isn't making them die, it is making them stronger.

As usual, it is all our fault but let us not point the finger of blame at ourselves, when it is much more satisfying to point it at officialdom instead. They do not make it difficult for us to do this. Sometimes, it looks like they are begging for it.

They certainly do not have to beg for their supper, as there will be an obliging banker or arms salesman along any minute to buy it for them.

Our government officials get taken to dinner by big business so often it is amazing they can find suits in their size.

There is nothing untoward going on here though, goodness me no.

Why would officials do favours for multinational corporations just because they treat them to a five star dinner, or take them to the best seats at Wimbledon, or give them some art or treat their other half and their children to the football, or the opera or an amusement park?

It is not bribery, it is just being nice.

And if you believe that, I have an organic, hand reared, free range, ethically sourced burger of mystery meat I would like to sell you.

18.02.18

If you have the money, the doctor will see you now.

In order to avoid a Brexit, David Cameron has been cajoling and persuading and threatening and pleading his European counterparts to give him something he can take to the people of this country to make it seem like he is getting a good deal for Britain.

That the people would not recognise a good deal for Britain if they fell over it in the street has not stopped him trying. He is very trying.

Of course, democracy is only allowed to go so far, and the *grands fromages* of the euro project do not want the notion that Britain is getting special treatment to infect the citizens of other countries, as it might cause them to demand the same.

Francois Hollande said "not on your nellie". He said it in French, so it sounded better.

Meanwhile, HSBC has just concluded a ten month review on whether they will move their operations to Hong Kong. They won't. I could have told you that. In fact, I did, many times when all this blew up.

The review was because of uncertainty about our future in Europe and also because David Cameron said he was thinking of being cross with the banks for their part in the downfall of the world economy and was seriously considering trying to prevent them from doing it again.

This caused the delicate souls on the banks' top floors to have a Victorian fainting fit and threaten to rush for the airport dabbing the tears from their eyes with a lace hanky.

It took them ten months to tell us what we already knew, that they would stay in exciting, vibrant London rather than move to some boring hell hole with nothing to do on their days off.

If the bankers really did leave, the crime rate would drop overnight.

In the Square Mile, they have not exactly solidified a reputation for financial probity and openness.

If you take our dependencies and overseas territories into account, the UK is the worst offender on the global financial stage for secrecy and aiding the laundering of ill gotten gains. We are literally a crook's best friend.

Do you have millions in drug money that you would like to wash clean? Come this way. Are you an African dictator that wants to take billions from the country you are supposed to be running and hide it in a safe place? Step right up. Would you like to avoid tax? Well, as long as it is a LOT of tax we are talking about, we are pre-eminent in that regard, please take a seat.

It is a bit rich for this government to be saying publicly that they are against tax avoidance and capital flight and the laundering of criminal fortunes, when they are simultaneously presiding over and protecting the most shady place on earth for those very activities, according to the Tax Justice Network.

Now the banks are saying that if we vote for a European exit, they will up sticks and flounce away to France, taking a thousand of their highly skilled screen watchers with them.

There is nothing like a banker telling you what to do to make you want to do the exact opposite, is there?

03.03.16

What's so super about it?

It was a Super Tuesday for companies that manufacture hair spray. They are going to have to increase their production because the Donald and a Hilary are going to be doing a lot of travelling and television, and they will need to look their best.

The latest results from America reinforce the feeling that we have all stepped through the looking glass and have arrived in La-La land.

Can you believe it? A six foot, bright orange Oompa-Loompa, with a candyfloss hair-don't, might become the most powerful man on earth. The whole world's gone crazy.

He took on the Pope and he won. He won in South Carolina and he won in Nevada, a state in which he was the second most garish thing, after Las Vegas.

His competitors for the nomination have had hundreds of millions of dollars thrown at them by billionaires who want the country run for their benefit. The sense of bewilderment that some foghorn off the telly is crushing that plan is palpable.

The Republicans are reeling.

The other candidates for the world's top job are now trailing far behind. Hard to believe that the American public have been left with these two. Nothing so ridiculous could ever happen in this country, of course.

In other news, our next general election will probably be a choice between Boris Johnson, a candy-floss topped, untucked buffoon, and Jeremy Corbyn, a man that I am sure used to teach geology on the Open University.

Think of it: the next meeting of the Special Relationship Club might be Donald Trump trying to understand what Boris Johnson is saying. We're doomed.

It won't be Prime Minister Jezza, of course. The Tories never tire of telling us how unelectable he is. This must mean they are scared that he might win.

J. C. has so disconcerted the establishment that they are reduced to sending David Cameron out to make supercilious, public schoolboy japes about the quality of his poor-boy suit.

You know they are rattled when they pick on your tailor.

Boris Johnson is a man who spends an awful lot on his suits and then purposefully dishevels them so as to maintain the image of a man who does not care about his appearance, and he has staked his claim to the top job in the Conservative Party.

Bozo the Mayor thought long and hard about what position on Europe would be most beneficial for him to take, and finally came to the conclusion that now might be the best time to bolt for the tape and grab the top job before George Osborne beats him to it.

The irony appears to be lost on him that a man who has spent his life pretending to be a dolt should now be asking the public to trust his judgement.

11.03.16

Wills and Wotsit - The Great Disappearing Act.

A feckless, work-shy couple have jetted off with their brood on yet another holiday on the taxpayer in some chavvy resort favoured by the Russian criminal class and given this country a two fingered riposte to the idea that they should work more and spend less.

Or...

The Duke and Duchess of Cambridge have taken their lovely children on a well earned break in the charming French mountain village of Courcheval, a favourite of the gilded jet-set, and have given the country a series of heart-warming pictures of the family for which we are truly grateful.

Wills and Wotsit are off on an additional break from their hectic routine of smiling and waving.

When David Cameron jaunts off, he regularly goes by the please-the-public holiday rulebook and travels on Easyjet.

The Cambridges went by private jet.

Will's godfather, the Duke of Westminster, is stratospherically rich enough to own one, due to his genius at acquiring not one but two O Levels and inheriting the really expensive bits of central London and much of the rest of the country.

So as to avoid meeting any smelly, needy, gawping members of the public, Wills made use of the Duke's plane to get to Courcheval. They did not alert the press that they were going and they only told us all that they had been when they got back. We did not notice they were away because they are practically invisible when they are here.

The Sun newspaper, which does a neat line in disapproving of the royal family while simultaneously strongly supporting them, reported that a senior royal source announced that the holiday was one that the royal couple booked and paid for themselves

Of course they did. Wills went through the exact same procedure as we do to book our holiday accommodation. He examined everything available on the net, compared and contrasted hotel rooms for ten hours before making a booking for the standard room, view of the car park, breakfast extra, no check in before 2pm.

The palace is trying to make it appear that they are just like us. They aren't.

On the seldom occasions that we have saved enough for anything more than a day in Scarborough, we plebs spend as much time organising and booking a break as we do actually enjoying one.

All the while we are booking it, we wonder if we are not spending too much and whether the hotel will be as nice as the pictures suggest. Or if it has been built yet.

This does not happen if you are second in line to the throne. Neither do you pay for any of it, and for the palace to protest otherwise makes them seem a little foolish. Or rather, it makes them look like they think we are foolish enough to believe it.

The jet they reportedly went on would cost about £10,000 to hire each day. Very expensive to those that can't afford it, free to those that can.

The place they stayed at will have been cleaned and refreshed to within an inch of its life and will have been provided for them for free, or at massive discount, as all accommodation is when you are a recognisable member of the royal family.

Property owners fall over themselves to provide the best that they have, so as to be associated with the Windsor brand.

The security that went out with them will be paid for by us, of course, at a cost of millions.

Just think - the bill for stationing two bored coppers outside the Ecuadorian embassy to make sure Julian Assange stayed inside cost about £4m a year, according to the Metropolitan Police.

Can you imagine what the highly trained and armed, expert shadowing force that the Cambridges have trailing after them comes to?

Then, of course, there will be the catering. The couple that ripped out a brand new, hand built £38,000 kitchen from their free mansion on the Sandringham estate and replaced it with one that was so expensive that the fridge alone cost as much as a semi in Liverpool, will require the finest wines and vittles available to humanity and they will want someone else to pay for them, as Wills doesn't do cash and I doubt he does credit cards either.

When they do slope off to a restaurant, as a break from the efforts of their private chef, they won't be waiting at the bar to be squeezed onto a table for two by the toilets.

The whole place will be cleared and they will have it to themselves. There will be more waiting staff than customers and it will smell of the paint the owners redecorated the place with when they heard they were coming.

made all that up. I don't know if any of that is true but would you be surprised if it was? The thing is, we have no idea because the whole thing was conducted under the utmost secrecy.

What's amazing is that the press went along with all this. The couple took one friendly photographer from the fourth estate to send back pictures of the happy couple, as a sop to the proles back home.

All other reporters and snappers were banned. And in the spirit of openness and free speech they went through this photographer's work and selected just six pics that they wanted everyone to see and no other picture was allowed to be published.

The various commentators could be put into two camps - there were the ones that are desperate for approval, possibly with an eye on a title, who fawn and fuss around their majesties' coat tails and gush about how simply marvellous they both are and what outstanding examples of fortitude and hard work and down-to-earth niceness they embody...and then there was the Daily Mail.

The Daily Mail may not always be on the side of kindness but I think they had it more or less correct when they railed against the increasingly walled off nature of the royal family.

The way in which The Firm are manipulating the press into publishing only stories that reflect well on them resembles the contracts that the papers must agree to if they want an interview with a big Hollywood star.

They sign away editorial control, and the stars want to be able to redact any passages they don't like and edit any photos that are taken. And that's all fine and dandy because they are not using our money to fund their fabulous lifestyles.

We can show our disapproval and correct their behaviour by simply not going to see their latest film, but there is no democracy with the royal family, we are stuck with them whatever they do and we are forced by law to pay for them regardless of their actions and how much work they put in to justify living the richest life of any family on the planet.

Bill Gates is the wealthiest man alive but he does not live as well as the Windsors. He does not have a selection of billion pound palaces with land in city centres to call his own.

The fact that the queen does not actually own them is irrelevant if she is the only one that can use them.

You could say the same about the soldiery she has at her disposal, the armed squads of silly hats on horses that clomp around at her command, the motorcade that makes the traffic stop, so that she doesn't have to.

And Bill Gates definitely does not get pensioners sitting by the roadside to wave a plastic flag at him when he speeds by on the way to an engagement.

The payback for this fantasy lifestyle is that we, the public are granted access. We want them to come and open things and cut ribbons and make speeches before we give them a free dinner and they take off in our helicopter.

We like the waving but we have to see them do it.

The point is that Wills doesn't. He only pretends to work as an air ambulance pilot. How many other people that do that job can show up when they want and then only for a couple of hours a day?

That's not a job, it is a hobby. Actually, it's not a hobby, it is a shield to deflect criticism from a young man who doesn't do much for the fabulous riches he has been gifted.

What he is really supposed to do is all that royal stuff which is now the purpose of the institution. He has had three so-called royal engagements in as many months. And a royal engagement can be just showing up for lunch and asking some specially selected someone if they have come far. It's not hard and he doesn't even do that.

We have an unwritten contract with the Windsors - we won't object too much if they get a ten million pound a year pay rise when we change the funding formula.

We won't mind too much if they pay their staff a risible wage for serving their every need and whim and we won't complain too much if we pick up the bill of hundreds of millions of pounds for security and so on, but in return we want them to do their bit, which these days is called entertainment.

As an incredibly well rewarded member of the royal family, we want them to stand there in the rain while a choir sings songs to them.

We want them to work the crowd and look pleased if some demented member of the public with green teeth pushes through to give them a pair of nylon slippers. We want to see them gratefully take some wilted posy from a child thrust forward by their parent.

In other words, we want them to act a little more like a Disney prince and princess, because that's what we pay for - the continuation of a fantasy which we throw a lot of money around to keep alive.

I can understand that the routine might not be something that a young man would want to engage in. Wills might hate the whole lot of it but that is the life he was born into.

Some people are born into poverty and homelessness and starvation. All things considered, we are not asking much in return for the fabulous returns.

So pucker up Prince William. Put your best smile on Princess Thingy. It is your job. Get out there among us.

There are less pleasant ways to earn a crust. You could be down the pit.

Or working as a butler for fifteen grand a year in Buckingham Palace.

18.03.16

Come on R2, drive my car

It used to be that the least reliable part of a car was the engine, then it was the electrics and now, the most unreliable component in the modern car is the dumbbell driving it

Pretty soon we will be relieved of the trouble of doing that and then we can concentrate on the things that currently take our eye off the road like when Ed Sheeran comes on the car radio and you have to change the channel RIGHT NOW, or you find an itch that you need to tie yourself into a sailor's knot to scratch, or you drive by someone on the pavement that you would like to have sex with.

That is great news - the sooner human beings are dragged from behind the steering wheel and it is replaced with a screen you can watch Police, Camera, Action! on, the better.

There is, however, a problem.

First they came for our computers, then they came for our phones, and now experts have said hackers will soon be targeting our cars.

Self-driving car technology is improving so quickly that some in the business believe that within the next five years we will be able to fall asleep on the motorway, just as we do now, but that it might not be fatal, and that means that we will be paying even less attention to the road. That means that hacking will be probably become a problem.

There is a thing called ransomware - it sounds like a mask you put on to conceal your identity when kidnapping someone - but ransomware is much more serious than that.

On a computer, it locks your machine down and won't let you back in until you pay a criminal in Russia three hundred pounds, which is quite upsetting if you are half way through watching the Game of Thrones episode that you just stole from the internet

It would much worse if the ransom you had to pay was for switching the controls of your car back on when you are doing 70 miles an hour on the middle lane of the M4 and you can't find your credit card.

Elon Musk is the man who invented cheese in a can, or something really big like that, and he told Fortune magazine that his Tesla Motors is two years away from achieving a fully autonomous self-driving car.

Experts estimate that by 2030, 25 per cent of all cars sold will be doing all the things we now have to do ourselves: tailgating anyone that is doing under 50mph on the High Street, leading the police on high speed chases through Essex and parking across two spaces, for example.

There are two scenarios that I can think of that might occur with ransomware. Either someone could lock you out of your car and ask for fifty quid to open the door...or they could take control of your car and drive it into a tree unless you transfer everything you have in your bank account to an address in Novgorod

One security insider said: "I'm not too worried about hackers who would try to hurt people by causing car accidents,"

He said: "In general, hackers are not interested in killing random people. It's also illegal to kill random people."

That's right, but it is also illegal to kill specific people, but that does not stop it happening every minute of every day.

The good news is that all of the companies developing self-driving cars take this threat very seriously, so when they do become available, self driving cars should be just as reliable as the computer on your desk!

25.03.16

The Answer Is: I Dunno. What's The Question?

EU news: if we leave, there will be an exodus of the most productive members of the economy. Expect a tidal wave of British bankers to wash up on the shores of a grateful Europe.

In other news, no bankers will leave Britain if we vote out.

I hope that is clear

In January of this year, the head of JP Morgan, Witherington T. Moneybags, said that his bank would quit the UK if we vote to leave Europe. That would mean 19,000 jobs going across the channel

Just a few weeks later, HSBC, the biggest bank in the world outside China, said that it would shift a thousand investment banking jobs to France if we vote to leave the EU.

They would leave the High Street operations in place, because it is quite hard to move a shop, and if we had to go to France to queue to see a teller, then we probably wouldn't bother.

Instead of waiting in line to deposit our cheques in a bank approved ultra-safe investment vehicle, we could enjoy the same returns by going to the council dump and throwing our money into the recycling bin instead.

In March, the chief of one of Britain's main asset management groups said that if Britain votes out, the pound will take such a hammering that we will be reduced to bartering with sexual favours and chickens

He didn't put it quite like that, I've gussied up his pronouncements a bit.

Meanwhile, several high profile investment banks have said that the pound could lose about 15% of its value if we leave.

Goldman Sachs said that banks, builders, property firms and home improvement businesses would be hardest hit if the UK left, and also predicted a slowdown in growth.

Research commissioned by the Confederation of British Industry said that a Brexit could knock 5% from the country's income and leave us in recession for years.

All that sounds pretty bad.

On the other hand, the prospect of bankers leaving the UK in the event of a Brexit are completely unfounded, according to the ratings agency Moody's who think that the two year window between voting to leave Europe and actually leaving would give us plenty of time to renegotiate our trade deals and so would not impact the economy that much.

HSBC have already decided to keep their headquarters in London, despite not knowing the outcome of the vote yet.

They examined the alternatives: Hong Kong (too hot), Luxembourg (too boring), Paris (too French) and decided that London was indeed the place where they would like to stay and enjoy what diversions their money can afford, which is a lot.

As for the economy, Unilever, Toyota and Nissan say leaving the EU won't affect their plans for the UK at all.

Boris Johnson and Nigel Farage are sure we should leave. David Cameron and Jeremy Corbyn are sure we should stay

Richard Branson says it would the worst decision the British public have ever made to leave the EU. John Caudwell, the founder of Phones 4U, says we would be better off if we quit.

On the one hand, it would be catastrophic for the economy for Britain to vote out in the forthcoming election...and on the other, it would be fantastic for Britain to vote to out in the forthcoming election.

And that does not even touch on the issue of safety.

To some people's disquiet, Nigel Farage did not waste any time after the Belgian attacks to say that they illustrate why we should leave, because of the ease with which terrorists can travel between European countries.

On the other hand, Theresa May and the former director of public prosecutions, and senior political and security leaders have said it is vital that we stay in the EU because of the cross border intelligence and policing that it allows.

Vladimir Putin thinks we should leave. Barack Obama thinks we should stay

With just months to go before we have to actually make our minds up, the polls are neck and neck.

They couldn't be any closer if they were Sellotaped together, and all the experts disagree, the economists are contradictory, business persons differ, politicians diverge, there is dissent on the Clapham omnibus, war in the press, and discord sweeps the land.

Only one thing is certain - everyone is guessing and no-one has any idea what they're talking about and if they say they do, they are lying.

When I say "lying", I mean that in a political sense. Politicians lie about everything all the time. "Lying" is just another way of saying "talking", and they have been "talking" a very great deal about Europe.

There are economic issues, political problems, safety dilemmas, planning considerations, transport matters, free movement arguments and jobs concerns .

Beware any politician who tells you they know exactly how any of these troubles would be resolved whether we voted in or out.

You might as well take advice from your dog. At least a schnauzer won't fiddle on its expenses. Piddle yes, fiddle no.

31.03.16

A Wave Of Un-migration.

There is an interminable wait until the nation gets to choose whether they like the lies that the "Better Off Out" or "Stronger In" sides are using to batter the public into doing what they want.

The 23rd of June seems like an age away. It will certainly feel like that as we are assailed every day from now on with scare stories and threats and promises of green grass or eternal damnation.

The intimidation and cajoling from the doom mongers and nay sayers will be a gauntlet that we have to plod through before we get to the point when the losing side will call it a fix and demand a re-vote.

The economy will fall or fly, society will crumble or coalesce and the future is bright or benighted. Other alliterations are available.

One outcome of an out vote has not had much discussion. Possibly, the public is unaware. The issue is a serious one and it involves people coming to this country and it is happening already.

The uncertainty of the referendum's outcome is causing a rush of incomers from places like France and Spain, Greece and Italy. They are coming at the rate of 100 every day. They are tanned and comfortably shod and they are complaining almost constantly.

They are the British ex-pats who decided that they preferred to spend their retirement where the sun shines but have heard they might not get health care if Britain leaves the EU, and they are rushing back to form an orderly, misanthropic queue at the GP's.

France has already said that Britons abroad will not get free health treatment if there is a Brexit. Not all of France, of course, just one French minister, and he said it in French so it sounded like an invitation to a romantic assignation.

When it was translated to the Sidneys and Enids on the Costa del Sol, those that had them in spat their dentures out.

We, who stayed in Blighty, are about to be overwhelmed with incomers. We, who stayed to make this country what it is today are about to be subsumed in a wave of sun kissed elderly sourpusses who will be furious at having to suffer the weather here just to get a hip replacement and a prostate check.

They will trundle back on their Motability scooters and pour their ire over everyone that has been suffering over here, while they have been over there, enjoying themselves.

On their return, they will say things like: "Well, I'd forgotten how cold it is...and grey, and we can't make paella like they do in Spain and the beer's all warm, and the coffee's like water and it doesn't stop raining, and the bread tastes like cardboard and the sea is freezing and the beer's warm and you can't get tapas here and the sherry is so expensive and the cold is playing havoc with my knees and the sun never comes out and the beer's warm and I miss sitting out at night and you don't get the sunsets here and you could avoid the Brits in Spain but they're everywhere in Margate and the restaurants are so pricey and have you seen the cost of houses and you can't get those nice cheeses and the buses are full of foreigners and the pasta tastes funny and why can't you get nice pastries here and the beer's warm and it never stops raining. Still, mustn't grumble."

It is not too late. We must build a wall. Maybe Donald Trump could get the Mexicans to pay for it.

07.04.16

Dave's Dad's Panamanian Two-Step.

It is the biggest release of horrifying information that we already knew since the last time we stood on a speak-your-weight machine.

A law firm in Panama has been acting in a completely legal way to do things that most people would assume would be totally illegal.

That is because most people do not understand the law. The law is whatever the person with the most money says it is.

Panama has so much money it's amazing it is still afloat. It is so stuffed with cash that it's a geological wonder that the entire country has not broken free of the north and south of America and sunk to the bottom of the Caribbean.

It is so chock full of moolah it beggars belief that the Panama Canal hasn't been squeezed shut.

Panama is where you would send your money if you did not want anyone to know you had it. What kind of person would want that? Well, everyone who has a lot of money, as it turns out.

"We don't pay taxes, only the little people pay taxes" is a phrase associated with a stretched-faced Manhattan "socialite" in 1989.

Since then, on this side of the pond, David Cameron has stated that tax avoidance is "wrong".

This is phrase he uses a lot when he is presented with a problem he has no intention of doing anything about. Why would he? It appears that tax avoidance is key to his family's wealth.

Cameron's father used the services of the Panamanian law firm to hide his wealth from a government that was not being run by his son at the time.

David Cameron put out an extraordinarily carefully worded statement that said he does not benefit from any off-shore funds or shady shenanigans like that.

The problem is, if he was gifted hundreds of thousands of off-shore pounds in his father's will, and he spent that money on assets, like property for instance, then he does still benefit from the increase in value of that property.

In all the furore, I think that fact has been completely overlooked.

It is no good saying that you do not, nor will not benefit from tax avoidance, if you have already spent the money and the value of what you bought with it keeps going up.

Her Majesty's Revenue and Customs had no idea about any of this.

The biggest release of secret financial papers detailing the exquisitely complicated way that the rich organise their affairs so as to avoid becoming one of the little people, took them completely by surprise.

Do not think that they will be as clueless or accommodating if we try to avoid paying *our* dues.

We are not remotely rich enough to be able to get away with it.

08.04.16

A Maximum Security Safe Space.

Students are a delicate sort, possessed of the notion that they know everything, because no-one has told them otherwise.

During their short lives, the modern parent will have cosseted them from taking responsibility for their actions, no matter how appalling.

Should any member of the public have shown irritation at their childish screaming in a crowded place, or complained at being hit in the face with a plastic toy while they are trying to read the paper on a train, their parents will have reacted with apoplectic, bug-eyed fury.

Absolutely everything that their little precious darling has ever done is super, and a modern parent will want to kill anyone who says otherwise.

In their children's school, everyone gets prizes. With their parents, every little thing they do is magic.

If you have spent your whole life being protected from failure or criticism or correction, then it is no wonder that when a dissenting voice is heard you explode with indignation.

This might explain the stories of rage that make up the parts of the newspapers that aren't telling us the sports results or selling us bingo.

Rage is an inappropriate response to an inconsequential action.

Everyone seems to be on the edge of going nuclear because there is a generation of people who have never heard the word "no".

At the Edinburgh University Students' Association, so delicate is their constitution that raising a hand to speak in a meeting is considered aggressive enough to warrant expulsion.

Imogen Wilson is the Vice-President for Academic Affairs of the Edinburgh University Students' Association. That is an actual post that I did not make up. At a student council meeting, she raised her hand to speak in disagreement with the person that had the floor.

This was perceived as aggressive and she was subject to a "safe space complaint". This is because students must not show disagreement in any way during one of their very important meetings.

There must be no raising of hands, or any other hand gesture that could be read negatively, and absolutely no shaking of the head. Unfortunately, Imogen did that too.

She was almost thrown out of the council. She is lucky they did not call the police.

Apparently, only gestures that are generally understood to indicate agreement are permissible at a meeting of the Edinburgh University Students' Association. This means that as primer for life in politics or business, being a part of the group is completely useless.

Playing non-contact football is not going to be much help if you ever get to play it for real and shielding any speaker from a critical gesture is no aid to future competence at the Dispatch Box, for instance.

That is what these student councils are for - preparing the next generation of politicians for the uneven road ahead. That is where many of our MPs come from. They learned their crafty craft from arguing in student union meetings.

Can you imagine what a grounding in safe space rules would do for the ability of a Prime Minister to command the House? Or be heard in it?

It looks like another great step forward on the road to infantilism.

Very young children may need safe spaces to express themselves without fear of contradiction. That should probably be gradually removed so as to prepare them for life.

That grown ups in their twenties are still demanding it is bizarre. Would they like some Farley's Rusks to go with their bedtime drink?

It is typical Edinburgh, by the way. This would not have happened at Glasgow University.

In Glasgow, it is permissible to headbutt someone in the face to express your disagreement...or simply to get their attention.

15.04.16

Shouting for victory.

The Dutch footballist and manager of Southampton FC, Ronald Koeman, has decried the modern player as being uncommunicative.

He said "We used to play cards on the bus to the match and go socialising and actually talk to one another".

He said it in Dutch, so it sounded like a cat coughing up a fur-ball.

Today's players are less interested in communicating face to face. Like most young persons, they prefer to interact on social media.

Unfortunately, social media is the least social thing that has ever been invented. You could communicate more effectively over Donald Trump's Mexican wall.

One of the major problems with social media is that everyone is on "send". It does not matter if you follow 86 million people on your Twitter account, the only person you are actually attending to is you.

This becomes a problem in the world of football because players are supposed to be constantly talking to each other during the game, so as to rally the troops, cover the bases and avoid the bunkers, or something.

You may have heard players interfacing with each other during a game. They will say things like "Dave...Dave...over 'ere", or "Oi, oi! Sergey, on me 'ed!!!".

Sometimes they will say "Ref...ref..open your eyes you ******* ****!!!".

Sadly, increasing numbers of players do not do this any more. They have more words tattooed on them than they exchange during a game.

They barely know the names of the people on their team as they have their headphones on and are staring at their phones right up until the officials check their boots for luminosity and they jog out onto the pitch.

As I write, Southampton lie a creditable seventh in the Premier league. Their manager thinks that they could be doing even better if they looked up from their screens and got to know their fellow team mates.

To that end, Ronald has concocted a task. He said that to encourage communication on the pitch, he is setting his players a training drill that entails performing two separate movement based tasks while chatting to another player simultaneously.

This is no small feat, however, they should be equal to it. That is why they get paid the big money.

How many times have you read of a Premier League player asking another for a condom, while pleasuring two ladies and filming the orgy on their phone all at the same time?

If only they could be as good on their feet as they are lying down, then the English football team could triumph at Euro 2016.

If our players communicated more on the pitch, we might not be sent out in the quarter finals by Germany, who talk to each other lot, in German, which I can tell you is a lot more difficult to learn than English, which I managed to pick up by the time I was two.

So come on boys, you can do it. Practice your multi-tasking.

Walk, chew gum and repeat after me: the lads done great, it's all credit to the lads.

22.04.16

Not Normal Naming

Is Cyanide a nice name for a girl? I am just asking because that is what a mother wants to saddle one of her new twin babies with. She wants to call the boy Preacher. He appears to have got off lightly.

With a little nominative determinism, he could eventually become Pope, or one of those people that live in the hills around Los Angeles who mix up the Cool Aid for their soon to be ex-disciples.

There is an epidemic of daft names being given to children. Old names like Enid, Ethel, Hubert and Godfrey may sound silly to us now, but they didn't when they were christened.

Some names may go out of fashion but some will never be in fashion.

Celebrities are at fault here. There is an arms race of silly names that the famous give their children, in what looks like an attempt to become famous-er.

It is look-at-me behaviour from those that want to make the point that they are so well off that they can send their little precious into the world called anything at all and still they will want for nothing.

Either that, or they were stoned during the christening ceremony.

Some celebrities might have chosen the names for their children for completely different reasons, but I can not for the life of me think what possessed Jamie Oliver to allow his children to be called Buddy Bear Maurice, Daisy Boo Pamela, Poppy Honey Rosie and Petal Blossom Rainbow. They sound like rejected characters from the Teletubbies.

Bob Geldof called one of his children Fifi Trixibelle, which would be fine as the name of a child's toy pony but will sound absolutely ridiculous on an adult: "Hello, my name is Fifi

Trixibelle and I will your pilot today. Dipsy Wipsy Lala will be your co-pilot".

That would empty the plane back out onto the tarmac in the time it takes to flick on the seatbelt sign.

It is not a new thing - Frank Zappa famously forswore drugs, so had no excuse when he called his son Moon Unit. David Bowie named his son Zowie Bowie and Donovan gave his the name Oriole Nebula.

Jermaine Jackson, Michael's brother, called his child Jermajesty. I am not making that up.

Coldplay's Chris Martin and Gwyneth Paltrow gave the name Apple to their first born. After their favourite fruit, presumably. Or their favourite phone.

Which brings us back to today and the mother who selected Cyanide for her daughter because she said it is a positive name as it was the substance that Adolf Hitler supposedly took to kill himself.

Every time that child would introduce herself in future, she would have had to explain the origin of her name to looks of bemusement or incredulity.

Thankfully she has been spared that fate by the courts who were alerted to her predicament by council care workers.

The mother has had five children to date, all of which have been taken from her, as she has a history of drug and alcohol abuse, relationships with abusive men and mental illness.

The court ruled that she should not be allowed to name the child Cyanide and she gracefully admitted defeat. Just kidding, she fought for her right to do what she wants.

She appealed. You might not think that she sounds very appealing. The Appeal Court certainly did not and the final ruling has come down that the little girl will not be named after the poison that killed Hitler.

That should be a lesson to us all. If you wish to call your little one something ludicrous like Bonjella Heliotrope, you should first take the precaution of becoming famous.

30.04.16

A tremendously classy development.

Donald Trump won all the presidential primaries in the five US states that voted on Tuesday last week.

The people did not vote for his policies because he does not seem to have many of those.

They voted for his charisma and because he's that bloke off the telly. The parallels with Boris Johnson in this country are spooky. Same hair, same laughs, same fame.

Donald vowed to make America great again, whatever that means, and to take the country back, whatever that means.

After the win, Trump called himself the Republican "presumptive nominee" which are the longest words with the most syllables that he has used in the campaign so far.

If you monitor his speech closely, as I have, you will notice that he almost never uses words that are longer than two syllables, with the exception of the word "tremendous", which he uses a tremendous amount.

I am not saying that he does not know any words longer than two syllables, it is just that he knows his audience, which doesn't.

The states that voted were Connecticut, Delaware, Maryland, Pennsylvania and Rhode Island.

After studying a map of the USA for at least ten seconds, I can tell you that they are all near The Donald's home state of New York, apart from possibly Delaware which I couldn't find because there was a big "DE" marked where I think the state is.

This local advantage will not apply in the next sates to vote, so the result is far from decided.

The party's national convention is in July and he needs 1,237 delegates to win outright and avoid a contested ballot.

If he does not make it over the finish line before then, the billionaires that run the Republican Party will try to steal the nomination for one of their paid-for puppets.

They once favoured a Bush, but he is out of the picture and their other favourites fell by the wayside long ago, so they will have to back Ted Cruz, who is liked by most of those in the GOP as much as they like herpes.

Considering that he is the party's best hope of defeating Trump, the grandees will not be pleased to know that Cruz will be appearing in a sex tape.

Not Ted himself, of course - no one wants to see that, not even Mrs Cruz.

A 21 year-old woman has became a viral hit for looking like him and is going to be paid £10,000 to star in a porn film.

Searcy Hayes, from Natchez, Mississippi, appeared on a daytime chat show. It is one of those programmes that features misshapen people shouting at each other while waving their arms about.

She was accused of cheating by her fiancée Freddie Green but viewers were more interested in Searcy's looks because of her resemblance to the Republican presidential hopeful.

A pornographic website reportedly became so excited that it offered Searcy and fiancé Green $10,000 to perform in an adult film.

The sex tape is to last for six minutes, which is probably longer than anyone will be able to stand to watch it.

Before she appeared on television, Searcy Hayes had no clue who Ted Cruz was.

She said "I don't know anything about him and I've never seen him and I don't know his positions", which is unfortunate, as she will have to come up with a least two for the video.

Her fiancée said: "I never had anyone say: here's $10,000, go make a sex tape. It's kind of exciting and shocking to know she's famous — she's more famous than Madonna!" "

That is not true - Madonna is much more famous.

And besides, Madonna did not make a sex tape, she made a sex book, which makes her more famous and classier too.

Tremendously so.

06.05.16

A XXX gift from the gods.

A day after a solar eclipse swept across Southeast Asia, Indonesian villagers thought they had been blessed by an angel fallen from heaven when a beautiful doll washed up on a beach.

Reports of a holy offering spread like wildfire through the community, after one of their number found the doll when he was fishing off the coast.

The expectation of divine blessing was increased as solar eclipses have a deeply spiritual significance in Indonesia.

In Great Britain we are not so easily amazed and associate eclipses with special editions of Blue Peter.

On the island where the Komodo dragon lives, when the sun became obscured by the moon, locals thought that a chariot had raced across the sky and blocked out our star and the gods sent a celestial being to bring good tidings, or some other such nonsense, who cares?

The doll was real, no doubt about that.

The man who found it took it to his home in Kalupapi village, where it was treated with the reverence and respect that it deserved.

It was treated as an angel and given a fresh change of clothes and a nice new headscarf to wear every day and pictures showed it sitting up in a chair, all life-like but inanimate, like something from a child's bedroom in a Stephen King film.

When the story of the heavenly marionette started to spread - that it was sent from the gods, that it cried and had human characteristics - police feared that social unrest might ensue so they went over to take a peek.

What they saw when they got there was a doll alright, but not any old doll, because this was a speciality figurine.

No ordinary puppet was this. This was a dolly with a unique purpose.

This was a blow up erotic aid. What they had dressed up in their finest finery was in fact an inflatable sex doll.

The police explained that the villagers were simple people, they had no television, they had no internet and so their minds had not become sullied by modern perversions.

After investigating, the officers confiscated the doll and took it to the local police station, a move they said was intended to stop false rumours from spreading.

Plus, they didn't want anyone else having a go.

12.05.16

An Accidental Slip Of The Truth

David Cameron was accused of an unforgivable lapse when he was overheard saying to the Queen that the incredibly corrupt countries of Afghanistan and Nigeria are incredibly corrupt.

This slip of the truth was met with howls of derision and complaints because when you are a politician, you are not supposed to tell the truth about people that are crooked, you are supposed to lie and say that they are not.

This particular form of lying is known as...diplomacy.

The fact that he said it just before an anti-corruption conference and it happens to be correct is neither here nor there. You do not get far in modern politics by sticking to the point or being accurate.

The fact that the Queen was listening to him at the time was somehow made to be the point of the furious response by the usual purple-faced royal hem sniffers who rush to protect a sturdy woman who doesn't need their help.

She has spent her whole life exchanging small talk with some of the most crooked people on earth.

An anti-corruption organisation called Transparency International makes a table each year of the world's most shady countries, with number one being the least bent, and out of 167 places, Nigeria is 136th.

Afghanistan is 166th - only North Korea and Somalia, tied at 167th, are worse in the whole wide world.

The tall blond people are the best by the way. Denmark, Finland, Sweden the Netherlands and Norway are the least corrupt, along with New Zealand, whose prime business activity is providing scenery for fantasy films - not much scope for corruption there.

The scale of the racketeering, extortion and crime is staggering. Just look at Nigeria, for instance.

Financial ombudsmen have had cause to fine them £284m for manipulating foreign exchange markets and then £233m for doing the exact same thing and fined them £226m for rigging the interbank lending rate and then fined them £225m for cheating on foreign exchanges and then they had to pay the authorities £221m for the same thing again and £217m for the same crime and then they got a £216m fine for doing it again and a £160m fine for a failure of risk management, a £137m penalty was paid for the same thing again and they were fined £126m for failing to protect its clients' assets.

Oh wait, that wasn't Nigeria, that was the banking community in the City of London.

I don't wish to use undiplomatic language but the truth is that London is a haven for the world's corrupt super rich to park the cash they've stolen. That's not me saying that, its Transparency International, which exposes corruption for a living.

They said that Britain's system of halting the flow of dirty money was shot through with holes - loop holes, if you will - and that British banks, British lawyers and British estate agents have made London the planet's prime destination for laundering money.

Isn't it handy that countries from all over the world sent delegates for an anti-corruption summit to London, where they would not have to travel far to see some of the spoils of that corruption?

It was being held in Mayfair. They could have all gone on a walking tour of nearby properties to see what that corruption has bought.

If they had invited some London banks along, they could have made it a how-to seminar.

16.05.16

PC's fail on PC.

Police have apologised for making a fake Islamist suicide bomber shout a well known catch phrase during a counter-terrorist exercise in Manchester.

This was a drill that tried to resemble as far as possible a terrorist attack so as to prepare the emergency and security services for a real one.

It was important to be as realistic as possible because the terror threat was recently raised from "Oh no" to "Arrrgggghhh!!!"

The simulated offensive started when a man dressed in black walked into the Trafford Centre and shouted "Allah Akbar" at the crowd and then pretended to blow himself up.

An explosion rocked the food hall and hundreds of volunteers,dropped to the floor or ran screaming into shops and cafes. They did that because if they had just continued sipping lattes and trying on chinos in The Gap it would not have been very realistic.

It was all going very, upsettingly well until community groups and activists condemned the use of "stereotypes" for the exercise.

"Can you pls explain why the terrorist in the exercise was Muslim?" one tweeted. "Why should it be a Muslim shouting Allah Akbar", said another.

Manchester University Diversity Officer Ilyas Nagdee said : 'Stupid decision by greater Manchester police to decide the attackers should be seen as Muslim".

They are all right, of course. He should have called out "Crackerjack pencil" before he blew himself up in case there is an attack in the future by a children's' television extremist.

Or perhaps he could have sang Happy Birthday or hummed the Antiques Roadshow theme tune, or shouted "Owzat" before blowing himself up to prepare us for a cricket related suicide terrorist outrage.

In response to the furore at the use of the phrase Allah Akbar, Greater Manchester Police's Assistant Chief Constable Gary said the decision was "unacceptable" and apologised for any offence caused.

He's right to apologise, because apart from this week in Munich when a man screamed 'Allah Akbar' and killed one passenger and seriously injured three more after knifing them at a commuter train station, it is virtually unheard of.

That is, unheard of except for the terrorists who shouted Allah Akbar during the Charlie Hebdo shooting in Paris, and in January Parisian Police had to shoot a man dead who tried to enter a police station armed with a knife, shouting Allah Akbar, and in the Bataclan concert hall in Paris, the attackers who killed 89 people and wounded 200 others shouted Allah Akbar, and the man who shouted Allah Akbar when he drove his car into crowds of people and ran down 11 in Dijon, France in 2014 and Allah Akbar being the war cry of Islamic State.

But apart from all that, I can't imagine why the Manchester police thought that it would be appropriate for the suicide bomber to shout it when they were trying to recreate the most likely terrorist attack.

It's mystifying.

20.05.16

Depressed? You Need A Fungi To Be With.

Imagine traipsing though a bosky glade, an opening in the trees on some light-dappled hill. The scent of myrtle in the air, the leaves on the trees a golden glow.

Amidst the tufted grass, touched by tears of morning dew, you spy a crop of mushrooms peeking out into the autumn sun.

If that is on one side of the hill, and you pick them and take them home and share them with the family, you have just found breakfast. If it is on the other side, you have just become a drug dealer and you will go to jail faster than you can spell "psychoactive".

That makes sense, don't it?

The natural organism that has been declared against the law is called a magic mushroom. Many scientific studies have shown their usefulness in helping treat people with the abject misery that can come with cancer. In America, therapists can legally give their patients the mushrooms to help with this.

That's America. In this country, the government has decreed that possession of this particular type of fungus is to be punished. There are other types that are poisonous and could kill you. Those ones are, of course, perfectly legal.

They don't mind if you die, just so long as you are not enjoying yourself while you do it.

A recent study has shone an unflattering light on this particular fight in The War On Drugs.

An hallucinogenic chemical called psilocybin, found in magic mushrooms, was given to patients with depression by scientists at Imperial College London. They induced intense psychedelic trips in 12 people using high doses of the 'shrooms.

A week after the experiment all the volunteers appeared to have been cured.

These were people suffering severe depression that had been previously untreatable with a variety of therapies and expensive prescription medicines. They were unable to get better and lived with a crippling condition that the medical profession could not help them with, but nature could.

Three months later five still had no symptoms of the condition at all.

Normally in scientific studies a control group is used that gets a placebo of some kind. In this case, the researchers said it would be difficult to do that as it would be obvious which group had been given the real thing.

They would be the ones mesmerised by the light playing off the corduroy in their trousers and transfixed by the tune of a doorbell chime.

When they published in the Lancet Psychiatry Journal, they said that the psilocybin is believed to cause relief from depression by targeting receptors in the brain but that it might also recreate the same feeling that people get when having an intense religious or spiritual experience.

About 350 million people worldwide are affected by severe depression and according to official figures the annual cost to the economy in England is thought to be around £7.5 billion.

About one in ten patients are resistant to treatment, so you would think that the government would be completely on board, keen to get these people help, fully signed up to save the country all that misery and all that money.

Of course they aren't.

The unfortunately named Professor David Nutt, who took part in the research, criticised what he called the "Kafkaesque" tangle of regulations and licensing requirements that had forced the team to wait 32 months before being allowed to conduct the trial.

They added it to the things that you are made to wait about three years for, alongside getting the potholes in your road fixed and finding an empty seat on the train to work.

Because of the delays and the hoops they had to leap through, Professor Nutt said "It cost £1,500 to dose each person, when in a sane world it might cost £30".

It is just that sort of insight and expertise that the government valued when they sacked him for saying things that they disagreed with when he was the Government's drugs advisor in 2009. They hired him for his experience and then fired him for using it.

Maybe the government were stoned at the time.

One of the research scientists said: "For the first time in many years, people who were at the end of the road with currently available treatments reported decreased anxiety, increased optimism and an ability to enjoy things."

That is great news for those lucky enough to have been chosen to take part, even if they did have to wait 32 months to be treated.

However, if you are reading this and you suffer from a debilitating, desperate misery, don't get your hopes up and expect the government to help out and make the lives of sufferers like you easier.

They would rather you stayed depressed.

28.05.16

The Life Of AN NHS Consultant: Tee Time And Tea Time

You know what the problem is with the NHS?

I am not thinking about too few nurses, although that is probably true, and I don't mean too little money, although that's a huge issue, and it's not that there's more of us and we are all living longer, although that's true too...no, the problem with the NHS is that consultants don't put in the hours.

The junior doctors have been negotiating with that nice Jeremy Hunt, and the last we heard, there was a major breakthrough in the issue of junior doctors' hours.

The breakthrough is that they are going to get the consultants to do some of them for them.

Consultants are set to lose their right to refuse to work at weekends. Union leaders are believed to have agreed to scrap the clause allowing senior hospital doctors to opt out of shifts on Saturdays and Sundays.

That is a great step forward to allowing the Government to plan for an NHS with supermarket-style opening hours that will give patients the same level of service every day of the week.

I'm sorry, that should read a "better" level of service every day of the week.

The last Labour government looked at consultants' contracts in 2003, and because of their genius and expertise at negotiation they gave them the right to refuse weekend shifts and at the same time increased their average pay by almost a third.

It was such a catastrophic screw up that consultants were being paid overtime rates of up to £200 an hour to fill in the gaps. Five per cent of all the money going on the NHS was being spent on their pay.

They got paid much more to do much less, and then the government wondered why there weren't enough doctors left to cover weekends and nights. It was because they were all playing golf, or asleep. Or both.

The contract stipulated that some senior staff would be on call, should a problem arise, but the problem with having consultants on call is that junior doctors don't want to call them.

Consultants are the ones that have the junior doctors' careers in their hands. They are their bosses. If you were at work at three in the morning on a weekend and something came up, would you want to call your boss at home, wake him up and tell him you can't cope?

No, neither do they.

There are lots of consultants who positively discourage their underling juniors calling them .

I've heard many stories about some junior doctor up to his elbows in a patient that is bleeding to death and the message goes out to the consultant on call and he or she just tells them to cope as best they can and they will be in to check on them in the morning

That is the problem with weekend and overnight cover in hospitals - it is being done by overtired juniors who do not have the experience to make some of the decisions, or administer some of the treatments required, and they are petrified of calling up their consultant bosses to admit that fact, and if they do call them they are often treated like idiots and shouted at.

I know of consultants in different fields that happened to have been there and had to ring on-call consultants on behalf of struggling juniors who have been told to cope, and only by being told by an equal will the on-call consultant bother to come in to save someone's life.

That is what's wrong with the NHS - consultants act like lords and don't deign to come in after office hours and leave their inexperienced underlings to carry on without them while they put their feet up at home and congratulate themselves on what a great deal they managed to squeeze out of the last Labour government.

That, and the fact that there's too few nurses, too little money, there's more of us and we are all living longer.

03.06.16

The Revolt Of The Little People.

Do you know who is really looking forward to June 23rd, when this EU thing will be over bar the shouting and the wailing of the side that loses?

There is a group of people that REALLY want the voting day to arrive, and they are hedge funds and investment banks.

They are practically bursting out of their bespoke suiting in anticipation of the day that we will all decide we can not be bothered to vote because it is too cloudy, or it is too sunny, or the cat didn't come home last night or we just flat out can't be arsed.

The reason they are so keen is that they spy an opportunity to do some good in the world. Just kidding, they are going to use it to make a lot of money.

Hedge funds and investment banks have commissioned their own exit polls, which they will keep secret, so that they can lay bets on the outcome and make even more money than they already have and so increase their bonuses which they will park offshore where no tax man will ever find it. You know, the usual.

They want to get the result before anyone else knows it so that they can make trades based on that knowledge and clean up.

I am pretty sure there is a phrase for that - using knowledge that only a few people know, that is secret from the market, to enrich themselves.

It is not "cheating" because they would never stoop so low and it is not "insider trading" because that is illegal and hedge funds and investment banks would never do anything like that, goodness me no!

I think the phrase I am looking for is: "being very greedy and using their position of vast wealth to make sure they stay that way at the expense of everyone else".

Yes, that's it.

The electoral rules, of which there are many, allow exit polls to be conducted on polling day so long as the results are kept secret until voting ends at 10pm.

That is an interesting clause: they must be kept secret. Secret from whom? Secret from you and me, because we are not allowed to bet on the result because we are the have-nots, and the have-nots must take their punishment and know their place.

The rules do not apply to the haves and the have-mores, of course. They get to do whatever they want.

One pollster told the Financial Times: 'Hedge funds have asked for exit polls and for hourly polls on the day. He said, 'Banks are commissioning polls for their own consumption that are never released.'

Another pollster said "People in the City are wanting a head start." As though they don't have a head start as it is. They are in a race with the rest of us and we are tethered to the starting gate. How much of a head start do they want? And how much do they want it?

They must want it quite a lot. A basic exit poll starts at around £500,000

A half million quid for some blokes with clip boards standing outside schools and church halls asking us which way we voted.

The money involved in commissioning such polls is as nothing, however, compared to the mountain of cash they can make if they get that information before anyone else.

They can make MUCH more than 500 grand betting on the outcome if they know the result before it is announced.

Unless, that is, the people who are asked outside the polling stations lie about how they voted.

Think of it - if everyone that is asked by an exit pollster told them the opposite of what they had done, then a lot of crooked swells in the city will plunge their money on red and it will come up black.

We could call it pay-back, or revenge, or just good fun.

Wouldn't you like to see some berk in braces go puce as he's just had to cancel the order for his new yacht because a lot of little people didn't tell the truth about which way they voted?

It won't cost us anything, it is not illegal, will take no effort and you will remain completely anonymous.

Let's deprive some bloated plutocrats of their new Bentleys. Let's disseminate misinformation on June the 23rd and stick it to the banker racketeers.

Let's lie for Britain. Who's with me?

10.06.16

Going to war in board shorts and flip flops.

Have you ever been to Ayia Napa? It is the sun drenched resort town on the south-eastern end of Cyprus, where tavernas serve tzatziki and souvlaki beneath sweet, flower laden olive trees in courtyards.

The gentle breeze comes in from the Mediterranean, the cypresses bend, the sand glistens and thousands of British teenagers rub up against each other in nightclubs before staggering outside to throw up and pass out in the road.

Three British party-goers, I will call them Lewis, Alex and James, because those are their names, emerged into the daylight after a typical lads abroad night out and decided to do something non-alcohol related and took a boat to go and be sick on some dolphins.

As a way of coming down and reacquainting themselves with the world, they went straight from a nightclub, at well past dawn, to sail and talk and squawk with the animals.

Everything was going very well, until they noticed, through the fog of their inebriation, that the boat was going a little further out than they had anticipated.

After miles at sea, it dawned on them that they might be aboard the wrong vessel, and that they were not going dolphin watching. But they were young and on holiday, with no pressing engagements, so how bad could it be?

Well, geography fans, guess what is 100 miles from Ayia Napa? It is not the sort of thing you think of when you jet off abroad. Most people do not consult an atlas to see what is near the place they are going, they just book it and hope that the pilot knows how to get there.

If they had glanced at the map, they might have chosen their boat more carefully because right there in front of them was the looming coastline of...Syria

They were all aboard the 9 o'clock boat to Hell.

Had they caught sight of craft laden with desperate migrants fleeing the murder and mayhem, going past them in the opposite direction, they might have been tipped off sooner. Even so, it is the sort of detail that it is possible to miss when your head is throbbing like it is attached to a pneumatic road drill.

Still, not all of Syria is exploding all the time, there are quite possibly safe parts untouched by slaughter. That may be so, but where they were going made Iraq look like Disneyland.

They were headed towards Homs, which has for years been taking a starring lead on a programme on the television known as The News.

Hundreds of thousands of people have been killed there and to make matters worse, it is not known for its dolphin sightings.

They arrived in a war zone wearing board shorts, sunburn and a hang over.

Fortunately, a kindly man called Vladimir Putin is orchestrating things down that way and a Russian military police-person emerged from a Russian military base to invite them all to stand still and explain themselves, which they did in down to earth language.

Lewis, or Alex or James said : 'The last club closed at 7.30am so we just powered through to our 9am boat trip and ended up blagging our way on to the wrong boat."

He said: 'It's the most f**king ridiculous story, isn't it? After hours and hours we turned up in this place and we were like, 'What the f***, where are we?', he said, "We went to watch f**king dolphins and we ended up in f**king Syria.'

A translator at the Russian naval base reportedly 'fell about laughing' on hearing this.

It is also reported that at least one of their mothers did not find the tale amusing.

I would wager that she would not have approved of much that happened on that holiday, but fortunately for the lads, none of the rest of their break was so eventful that it appeared in the national press.

(Update: we found out later that this story was apparently made up as a prank but in a post-fact world where everything is true if you want it to be, I would quite like this story to be true, so it is).

17.06.16

I'll set your pay, and you can set mine.

There is an incentive that you have for going to work and doing a good job while you are there. Your wage is what gets you up in the morning and propels you to work and makes you put in the hours, or rather it is the thought of losing it that makes you do all that.

When you get to the exalted position of upper management, however, and you start to earn the big money, it is not the wage that motivates you at all. When you ascend to the heights of the boardroom, you apparently need to be motivated MUCH more than by a mere wage, and that is where bonuses come in.

We know that the wage alone is not enough to make upper management put in a hard day's work because whenever anyone like a shareholder criticises the amount of management bonuses, the answer is always the same - it is that they need to be incentivised.

BP faced a shareholder rebellion over executive pay in April, when nearly 60 per cent of shareholders rejected the oil giant's remuneration report, which awarded boss Bob Dudley £13.8million.

Recently, more than a third of shareholders in advertising giant WPP refused to back boss Martin Sorrell's £70million pay deal and it was accused of a 'history of excessive pay.'

There was a survey for consumer group Which? that looked into the trains service that millions of people have to take to get to work and it found that the company Go Ahead's trains were the worst value for money. Its trains were also voted the least clean and least punctual and the most difficult on which to get a seat.

Three Go -Ahead franchises, Govia Thameslink Railway, Southeastern and Great Northern, were voted the UK's worst.

David Brown is the chief executive of Go-Ahead and so you would expect that his remuneration would be rock bottom and would have stayed that way for years because of his company's reputation and performance

Of course, you would be wrong. He was awarded more than a 100% pay rise.

In 2013 he made the not inconsiderable sum of £924,000, last year he got £2.163m for running the worst railway company in the country, according the the poor sods who have to travel on it.

The housebuilder Persimmon was criticised this week by one of the group's investors that said their executive pay plan was a bit steep when they saw that senior managers were going to share a £600million bonus pot.

The chief executive of Persimmon will pocket around £100million all for himself. When this was questioned by the shareholders - the people that actually own the company - the housebuilder said that the sum was "designed to drive performance".

You would have to be the laziest person that has ever existed if you needed a £100m bonus on top of your huge salary to drive your performance.

Apart from the banking racket, the Persimmon house builder's executive pay plan is one of the largest ever at a FTSE 100 company.

Persimmon said: "This is a long-term plan which is designed to incentivise the management to deliver the capital return, grow the business and increase the share price".

It is a measure of how utterly divorced these people are from reality and any measure of justification that they could say out loud that their highest employee needs a bonus of £100m, on top of his salary, to do a good job.

Most people's incentive for doing a good job is that they will be fired if they don't, but when you get to management level, you can be a complete cackhanded buffoon and you still won't get fired.

At worst, you will get to spend more time at home counting the pile of cash they gave you for your golden goodbye.

It's not like the housing sector hasn't had help. Interest rates have been rock-bottom for ages and there are various government schemes aimed at encouraging construction because of the shortage of houses - so their performance has been given a hand by circumstance and by the government, using your money.

As you can imagine, because they are doing very well, the company wants to reward all those people who have made it possible by humping bricks and laying pipes and wiring homes and putting on roofs and digging up earth...you know...the ones that have actually got their hands dirty and broken a sweat to make it happen.

Just kidding, only a few men with white collars and clean finger nails get bonuses.

Construction companies pay their brickies about £8 and hour and labourers get around thirteen grand a year. The workers obviously do not need motivating like management does.

Those in the top jobs pay themselves these amounts because they can.

When they are lucky enough to get to that level, and it is mostly luck, they set their own pay, with the connivance of their peers on remuneration committees which set pay high because it sets a precedent that will be cited when those same people on the remuneration committees negotiate their own pay awards.

It is a tight little round of mutual pleasure giving.

On the upper floors, it's one long motivational executive circle jerk.

27.06.16

Put it away Helmut.

If you go down to the lake today, you are not in for a big surprise, or even an average sized one.

Bratwurst is off the menu at the Familiensport-und FKK-Bund Waldteichfreunde Moritzburg nudist group, who have been told to put it away.

The German nudists have been instructed to cover up because a refugee shelter overlooking their colony opens next month.

They are very big on nudism in Germany which is odd considering what most Germans look like with their clothes off. Much like us as a matter of fact: lumpen, podgy, wibbly-wobbly.

For over 100 years the Familiensport-und FKK-Bund Waldteichfreunde Moritzburg nudist group members have been getting their members out at a secluded campsite around a lake to the north of Dresden.

Since 1910, the naturists have enjoyed the feeling of the air and the clear refreshing waters playing about their personal parts, unhindered by constrictive clothing. Now, they have been ordered to squeeze themselves into a cozzy to go swimming, assuming they can find one that comes in their size.

This new "No Skinny-dipping" rule has been brought in by the local authorities because of the imminent arrival of the refuge residents of a new £1.2million facility.

They have fled the horror of war zones, they have seen their compatriots die, they have left their families and their homes are in ruin but they will apparently all go into a Victorian lady's fainting fit if they so much as spy some Bavarian's bits.

The instructions are clear, however, and they have been sent to the nudists on a laminated board, so as to protect them from getting wet, or sticky.

The Germans claim their nudist way of life is being threatened and they point out that the refugee centre is for men only, so it is not as though any women from cultures that frown on them having sexual thoughts might cop an eyeful.

The male refugees will most likely either be completely uninterested or they will be stationed by the lakeside with a pair of binoculars and a box of popcorn, so why the big to-do?

Local officials insist that the nudists will still be allowed to walk around their club area naked and a large privacy screen will be erected to help put everyone at ease.

They are going to have a large erection at the nudist centre.

If only Benny Hill were still alive.

30.06.16

The Devil's in The Small Print

Since the referendum, the value of the top 250 British companies fell by an unlucky 13%. Banks and housebuilders - two of our most valuable contributors to the economy - tanked, the pound fell to a 31 year low against the dollar, house prices have already taken a hit and the nation has had its credit rating downgraded twice in one week,

Those downgrades are important as they mean that borrowing money will cost the government more, which means the interest payments will take up what could have been spent on...oh I don't know...the NHS for instance.

The prospect of another recession is being talked about, tax rises and more austerity are considered the most likely future.

On top of that we have had the main Leave leaders rowing back on the promises that people thought they were voting for.

The promise was made that we would not have to follow EU rules or pay in, but that has been debunked by EU leaders who have said that we can't have access to the market if we don't contribute financially or allow free movement of people.

We knew that anyway, or at least the clever politicians did that were trying to pretend that we would get some special British deal that would mean we could cherry pick the bits of the EU that we like and discard the rest. They knew that was not going to happen but they did not want you to know that.

Chief Leaver Daniel Hannon has said that leaving the EU does not mean the numbers of people coming to Britain will be slashed and says the Vote Leave campaign never said it would.

It is classic read-the-small-print stuff. The campaign said "we will never get immigration down to the tens of thousands if we are inside the EU"...what he is now saying is that does not mean we will get immigration down to the tens of thousands if we are *out* of the EU...just that we wouldn't get that *inside* the EU. Sneaky, eh?

Boris Johnson has already said that we won't be stopping immigration. He even said that the referendum was not about immigration. Well Boris, tell that to the millions of people who thought that by voting to leave they would have less foreigners surrounding them in the bus queue.

He also said that he was glad that the pound was stable, while it was crashing to its lowest value since the 1980s, and he was pleased that stocks were rallying while banks stocks crashed by a half and we stopped being the fifth largest economy in the world and were overtaken by France.

Then there was the Vote Leave website which has now amended that claim that an exit would allow us to spend an extra £350m a week on the NHS. Nigel Farage said it was a mistake to offer that (of course, he waited until after the referendum to admit it).

Top Brexiteer Ian Duncan Smith has said the NHS claim was never a promise, and here comes the small print again, he said, "There was talk about it going to the NHS but it was never the total."

Of course, that wouldn't look so good printed on the side of a bus.

To sum up: the leavers said talk of the economy suffering was fear mongering, they said that there would be fewer immigrants, they said there would be more money to spend on vital services, they said that we would not have to follow EU rules.

It is hard to find any Brexit leaders now who admit to making any of those claims. Makes you wonder where they all came from.

Are you getting the feeling you've been conned?

01.07.16

The Baby Boomer Report Card. They Get An F.

A baby boomer is a person that was born in the years following the second world war, that thing that all those black and white films on afternoon telly are about, the thing that makes boomers go all misty eyed, despite the fact that they weren't there when it happened.

The boomers, who are 60 to 70 years old today, have had control of the world since they became adults in the sixties and their report card is in, so let's see how they have done.

Well, they failed to allow for an increase in population despite the fact that it has been very slowly growing all the time they have been in power and that they were responsible for most of it.

They failed to build enough schools and failed to provide enough health care, or houses. The future was rushing by them and they failed to prepare for it in any meaningful way and they have ruined the economy, not once but several times, as though they were just getting in the practice.

On their watch they have polluted the sea and the air and the land. You would have thought that it would have been hard enough to do just one of those things, considering how much land, sea and sky there is, but the baby boomers have managed all three.

Like all of the catastrophes they have wrought, the consequences will be felt not by them so much as the generations that come after them - their children and their children's children.

They knew that but they preferred not to think about it because if they did, they might have had to do something about it, which would have been expensive and inconvenient.

They bought their houses when they were giving them away free with ten gallons of petrol and just sat there while they shot up in value ten fold and then congratulated themselves on their genius at making money.

Houses that the baby boomers purchased for ten grand in the sixties are now worth a fortune, which is great for them but hell for anyone trying to buy one now.

Today's young won't have to suffer their fate too long, however, because it is the first generation in history that will die earlier than their parents.

This is because they were brought up on a diet of sugar and microwaved food-like products because it saved time that their parents could use to watch the Generation Game, collect Green Shield Stamps and fill out the football pools.

On the baby boomers' watch there has been a massive shift in the wealth of the nation from the many to the few.

In the sixties, the bosses of large companies typically earned 20 times the pay of the average worker. Today those CEOs have awarded themselves more than 300 times the pay of the average worker.

Between the 1978 and the year 2000, the average worker's real pay went up by 1%. The average Chief Executive Officer's pay went up by 1270% and the same thing happened again between 2000 and 2014.

The top boomers even managed to give themselves massive pay rises when the companies they were running and the economy in general were tanking, and if you think that is typical of the top 1%, it isn't.

CEOs of major companies have been allowed to give themselves pay rises 5 times higher than the top 0.1%, which means that the wealth has not been taken from the 99%, it has been taken from the 99.9%, which is practically everyone.

Boomers are also the last generation that will enjoy a comfortable retirement. Final salary pension schemes are a thing of the past.

Young people are peddling so furiously to keep up they haven't any extra to save for their retirement because they're spending it all on putting a roof over their heads because of a housing shortage that has not been addressed despite the fact that the population has only gone up by 0.4% a year since 1960.

Hardly an overwhelming increase unless you don't do anything about it for decades, but that would have cost money and required planning, so it didn't happen

Baby boomers even failed to plan to keep the lights on. There is a looming crisis in energy production in this country, and the nuclear power stations that we need to keep the toaster working and the TV on are now looking like they won' t get built because the French, who we were asking to construct them for us, along with the Chinese, are thinking of pulling out because of the Brexit vote.

Young people should buy shares in candle making companies if they have any money, which they don't because their parents crashed the economy again

All that - the pollution, the wealth inequality, the housing crisis, the lack of schools, the crumbling of the NHS, the economic carnage, the lack of planning is all down to one thing: short termism.

Baby boomers like to think that the younger generation are the most self obsessed and selfish generation in history but that is not true, because *they* are.

Boomers didn't want to pay more taxes, so the health service has fallen on its face and the energy infrastructure is completely overwhelmed. They could have used cleaner technology that would not have polluted the planet to the extent that they actually changed the weather the whole world over, but the cost of things would have gone up, so they didn't.

Politicians knew that they would not get voted in if they said more taxes would lead to a better and more equitable life, such as the Scandinavians enjoy, so nobody made a fuss.

You might say well, what could they do? What could the little people of the baby boomer generation have done to stop all that?

Well, they were there when it happened. If not them, then who? Were they waiting for someone else to come along to sort out their mess? And if so, it looks like they have finally found them. It is their grandchildren who will have to do that.

The baby boomers have done whatever they wanted to gain the maximum pleasure for themselves in that moment, crossed their fingers and hoped for the best while enjoying the fact that they won't be the ones that will have to pay for it.

And as a last two fingered salute before they go to join the great bus queue in the sky, they have set the course of the ship Great Britain away from Europe, a direction that the young specifically said they do not want to go, broken the rudder and repaired to lifeboats to set off for a glorious sunset while behind them their kids are bobbing about, engines stalled, on a sea of discarded, floating, plastic crap.

12.07.16

The Dangerous Games

The festival of sex and drugs that is known as The Olympics is about to come around again and the slogan of the Rio games is: "What's that smell?"

Just weeks before it is about to start, a strange odour is emanating from the sea off Rio's beaches, the cause of which is turning sailors' boats brown.

Experts say that sewage leaking from hospitals into the city's waterways has created a new 'super-bacteria', in the exact spot where open-water competitions will take place.

One competitor said it left her boat 'looking like a toilet'.

Waste from hospitals and hundreds of thousands of households pours into drains and streams which cross Rio, before it is sensitively processed by being poured directly into the ocean.

A Paralympic sailor said he keeps his mouth and nose closed at all times to avoid swallowing any water. Not breathing is an essential part of the training for these games.

Sailors taking part in test events earlier this year said they were colliding with floating debris, which it was impossible to avoid. One said the slick filled part of the bay staining her boat from bow to stern.

He said, 'The boats were completely brown, but the worst thing was we saw a lot of dead fish", and that is the difference between us - I would not say that dead fish was the worst thing, I would still be concentrating on the brown.

The colour of the bay is not the only thing that is concerning the athletes and spectators going to Rio - there is the very real possibility that there won't be any golf.

Apparently, golf is considered an Olympic sport, and that noise you can here is ancient Greeks revolving in their burial tombs.

How can a pastime that old people use to while away the hours before Countdown comes on possibly be considered an Olympic discipline? It used to be that Olympic sports were all about the skills of waging war and gladiatorial combat: running, swimming, throwing weapons, fighting, ice skating.

In order to get the punters in, expand the television coverage and to make more money, the Olympics now cover almost every endeavour known to man. This year they are making hailing a taxi an official sport.

Unfortunately, these golfers don't seem that bothered about going because they have used the excuse of the Zika virus to say they can't make it.

Other athletes that don't earn a hundred million pounds a year are still going because it is the thing they have been training their whole lives for, but if you are so rich Donald Trump pays you to play on his course, why take the risk of going to Rio where there's no prize money?

Despite the troubled waters and the virus, most athletes and governing bodies are desperate for the games to go ahead - the athletes have been training for at least 8 years for this moment and the organisers can not see past the mountain of money they would lose if they called it off.

After all, the water won't harm you as long as you do not get any on you or in you, and the

Zika virus can only cause abnormal births, paralysis, nerve damage and death.

For their part, the Rio organizing committee officials say everything is fine and World Sailing, the governing body of the sport that will use those brown waters, said it was 'not in a position to comment'.

It is difficult to comment when you are keeping your mouth and nose closed.

16.07.16

Happiness the Danish way.

Research from the World Bank shows that middle income people from the developed world are the only people on earth that have not benefited from globalisation, a process that started when the first caveman outsourced his wall painting job to the talented artist in the next valley.

Globalisation happens when people and countries interact and integrate. Lately, this has meant that everything we consume in Britain is made somewhere else.

Before globalisation, we had to make do with goods that were manufactured in this country, which is why our cars always broke down and our clothes came apart at the seams in the bag on the way home from the shop.

The very poorest people on earth have had their lives changed by this interconnectedness.

The Chinese, who were living an agrarian existence, planting rice in some of the most beautiful scenery on earth, are now making mobile phones they can't afford in windowless sweatshops for 14 hours a day. Their lives have changed but whether it is for the better is debatable.

What is indisputable is that they have become wealthier. Now they can afford the magazines that advertise the things they haven't got the money to buy yet.

In the West, the people in the middle income bracket, that is those not homeless or on benefits but not in the process of moving to Monaco for tax reasons, have not benefited financially from globalisation at all.

Actually, it is worse than that - the vast majority of the first world's population have actually had a pay cut, in real terms, over the past twenty years.

The poorest in the world have seen their circumstances improve, financially speaking, and the richest have done fantastically well, thank you very much, but those in the middle have been screwed.

The World Bank researchers call it the most profound reshuffle of people's economic positions since the Industrial Revolution.

It might also be viewed as the biggest transfer of wealth from the masses to the elite in modern history.

There is also the small matter of the enslavement of the poorest who now make all our stuff, for a pittance.

Alongside this has come the celebritification of the media. The lifestyles of the rich and shameless are paraded in front of us every day. Indeed, we seem to seek them out as some sort of glorious self-flagellation.

On television, in cinema and magazines and on social media the richest and thinnest and most beautiful waltz through their gilded lives showing off the wealth that globalisation has brought them, while the rest of us have our noses pressed against the window, wondering why we aren't getting any.

This is probably why there is a movement to the edges in societies across the world. Countries that have been stable in their middle-ground political leanings are now seeing the emergence of the far right and left.

It also might be why the world's Happiness Index is on a downward curve, except in the Scandi countries. Denmark in particular is always at the top of such lists.

It might be because they have a more caring society that is not so obsessed about the demonstration of wealth and status. They don't feel the need to define themselves by what they own as much as those people in less happy countries.

Of course, it also might be because they are all six foot and blond and get to have a lot of hot Danish sex with each other.

We should get the World Bank to look into that.

They could produce a report with illustrative pictures. Wouldn't that make you happier?

23.07.16

All Aboard The Urine Express.

You know when you are out and enjoying a nice cup of tea and some mouth breather's children are screaming and screaming and screaming and running up and down and crashing into things and generally acting normally for British children these days?

A lady who runs a cafe in Felixstowe has come to her customers' rescue and politely informed the moronic parents of these moronic children that if they can't deal with their issue then she will correct them herself.

Well, as you can imagine, when the internet heard about this it was awash with compliments and appreciation

Just kidding - everybody who is in possession of a child went absolutely, clenched fist, purple-faced berserk.

They said, "Dahnt choo tell me baaaht my kids, it's their right, they can do what they want", or words to that effect.

The cafe owner is called Kim Christofi (not affiliated to Kris Kristofferson) and she put on her Facebook page the following perfectly reasonable message, that in a more civilised place and time she would not have to have written at all, it said:

'Can we make ourselves perfectly clear to all parents who are too scared to discipline their children about tantrum screaming?
'We will give you five lenient minutes to ask the child to stop screaming and then we will ask the child ourselves.
'If that means you too having a tantrum about our having to speak to your child and hurling threats about not returning – that's really okay with us. We have a duty of care to the rest of our customers.'

She underestimates the public's inner ire and total belief in their own self-worth. The threats wouldn't stop at not returning, they would go all the way up to stabbing her, burning down her cafe and blasting off and nuking the entire site from orbit.

And that is the problem. Children learn that behaviour from their stupid parents who let them run around and scream their heads off like chimps in a zoo because every little thing their precious does is magic, and anyone who says otherwise will see the sharp end of their parents' insane, bug-eyed, demented, infantile fury.

You see this everywhere. I was on a packed train this week leaving Clapham Junction. People were standing shoulder to shoulder all down the aisle, no seats to spare on the hottest day of the year and one family that were behind me were making a hell of a noise.

I turned round to see a completely naked child jumping up and down on a seat next to her mother who was on the phone talking loudly to someone about how the shops have air conditioning in them down here, like she'd just taken a train from the 1960's.

Meanwhile, her small naked offspring, which seemed to be being wrangled by her other slightly older child, starts peeing on the floor. A woman gets out of the seat opposite and chooses to join the crush standing up instead. The mother does absolutely nothing about it whatsoever.

The child in charge lets the younger one finish, takes him back on her lap and then says, "Ohmygod, is that sh*t?"

Just so you know, they were sitting with their backs against the train toilet, but to use that would have entailed them getting up, so obviously that was out of the question.

What kind of adult is this child going to be?

If you grow up not having any boundaries or limits to your behaviour and anything you do is celebrated and violently defended by your parents, what are you likely to become?

A leading scientist perhaps, a top surgeon, or a guest on the Jeremy Kyle show?

30.07.16

The aerial pleasure delivery system.

Amazon has won approval from the Government to lift strict flying restrictions so that it can start the process of delivering by drone the things you don't need that you bought with money you don't have.

That means unmanned flying machines criss-crossing the sky with no human control.

What could possibly go wrong?

The Civil Aviation Authority usually has strict rules that govern drone pilots, like maintaining sight of the vehicle, not allowing it to enter private property and not being stoned while driving it.

The CAA has waved many of these rules for the internet giant, just as the governments of the world have waved the necessity for it to pay the same rate of tax that bricks and mortar shops do by putting in more loopholes in the law than you would find on your granny's cardigan.

Amazon wants fleets of drones delivering small packages directly to your door within 30 minutes of you making the mistake of ordering them.

The little, fleeting joy of receiving what you ordered in less than a few hours will probably increase the likelihood of you buying things because the reward will be almost instant.

They are training us like Pavlov's dogs - we hit the bell and get a treat. The positive feedback of pressing "Buy Now" online and having the package delivered that afternoon will be much more powerful than going to the shops or waiting a week for delivery.

On the high street, the purchase is immediate - you pay and walk out with the goods there and then. There is none of that delicious torture of anticipation of waiting to get what you want.

When ordering online and then waiting for a week or two, the sensation of collecting the parcel from your front door is too far removed from the action of buying to associate the act of purchase with the prize.

A delay of a few short hours, on the other hand, is just enough to arouse expectation and reinforce the connection between buying and receiving.

It is genius.

We in the UK are the ones to have been selected to have the most extensive trials of Amazon's drones anywhere in the world. Aren't we lucky? We will be lucky to have any money left by Christmas.

The flying robots will take off from the warehouse vertically, then move to aeroplane mode in the sky and hurtle their way to your area to land vertically.

It's not science fiction, it's science fact. Less sci-fi, more sci-fa.

They will just load it up and set it free to wend its way to you, when, if it behaves like human postal delivery workers, it will leave your package at the neighbour's, or an address that looks like yours but isn't.

Or it will leave a message that says you were out when it called and your package is on the roof.

It is the future, and the future is now, and it is so bright you will need shades.

You could buy some on Amazon, and factory workers will carefully package them up and place them aboard your delivery drone which will deposit them in the road outside your house where they will get run over by one of Elon Musk's driver-less cars.

07.08.16

Automation: the key to happiness.

Ricky Ma Wai-kay, a name I am not making up, has built a life-sized robot that can be used for sexual gratification, presumably by Ricky Ma Wai-kay.

The bot is reported to have cost £37,103, which seems an oddly specific amount, but that is because it was a round number of Hong Kong dollars, exchanged into pounds at the current rate.

Ricky could have bought a car for that amount, but you can only have sex IN a car and not with it, so it seems like a sensible decision. Besides, he sees the potential for the nascent mechanical mating industry and he wants to be on top, so to speak.

This android making visionary is certain that realistic bedroom droids will be big business in the future and thinks that they will become a part of every normal home.

Abnormal homes may also want one.

To operate the droid you speak to it through a microphone and ask it one of a set of questions, like: are your nodes warmed up? Or: may I upload something onto your interface? That sort of thing.

I forgot to mention the best part - Ricky Ma Wai-kay has made his love machine in the spitting image of the actress Scarlett Johansson, who is over the moon.

Who wouldn't like the idea of their exact likeness being used for the personal pleasure of a man they never met and would probably cross the street to avoid?

There is a video online showing the Scarlett Johansson sex-bot thanking its owner when he compliments it and giving him a wink. That is not a misprint.

As you can imagine, building this thing was not all plain sailing. There were problems ranging from burnt-out electric motors, to the robot losing its balance and toppling over, but that is to be expected with vigorous use.

This story first emerged a few months ago but is newly relevant because a survey about pleasure droids was recently conducted and found that one in five British people, who expressed a preference, said they would have sex with a machine.

The same poll revealed that one in three would go on a date with one, which means that a large number of people would date a robot but they would draw the line at having sex with one because, you know, that would be crazy.

Of the people that would actually make out with an automaton, three quarters said they thought that the robot would be good at it.

In the future, robots will probably become so expert that they will most likely only want to have sex with other robots.

That will restrict us humans to having sex with each other, but it is because that was so unfulfilling and difficult to find that we invented bionic bedroom aids in the first place.

That same survey also suggested that the reason we would most like a sex-bot, is for it to do the cleaning.

How fabulously British is that?

15.08.16

Crisis? What crisis?

You will be aware that this country is in an extremely serious economic position. It is so severe that Theresa May's first act, on taking the reigns of power, was to immediately go on holiday.

If you go down to Westminster today, you're in for a big surprise. The whole country is teetering on the brink of ruin and there's no-one there.

They have all gone to Europe to spend seven weeks planning their next holiday, which they will take immediately on their return. They will not call them holidays, however, they will call them "fact finding missions".

It is a complete coincidence that these missions seem always to be to fabulous holiday destinations.

To get to go on one of these trips, an eager parliamentarian must first volunteer to be on a Commons Select Committee.

You may have seen one of them at work on the telly just recently, sitting round a horseshoe table on fancy green chairs, having their questions batted away by a round man with a yacht tan.

You may have wondered what is the point of a parliamentary select committee if they can not even lightly grill that BHS man who looks like he just emerged from the oven, basted in his own juices, ready for the Christmas table.

The point is that there are lots of such committees and they have to get to the bottom of their chosen subject.

They could do this by picking up a telephone and discussing the issue with experts in other places, or they could carefully select those people they wish to communicate with and visit them in person, based on the desirability of the location they are in.

Austerity is an unknown concept in select committee land. Last year the bill for such trips was £430,000, this year they spent £550,000. That's about a 25% increase, maths fans.

They spent all that public money going to marvellous places with five star hotels and much for the visitor to see, such as Washington, New York, Boston, Italy, Copenhagen and a greyhound race track. Some of our MPs have gone to the dogs.

What do they do to justify their all-expenses-paid jaunts abroad? Nine MPs of the International Development Committee spent £35,667 on a trip to Washington and New York last September to look into "sustainable development goals".

I have no idea what that means. I wonder if they do? Might it just possibly fly in the face of sustainability goals to burn a hole in the planet's ozone layer jetting across three thousand miles to talk about it?

That same tanned group also went on a £44,000 five day visit to Nigeria at the end of February to investigate how British aid was being spent.

Apparently, it is being spent on determining how it is being spent.

It gets worse - eight members of the Defence Committee went through more than £50,000 on a six day trip to Washington.

That is £6250 each, for 8 days away.

Have you ever spent £6250 per person for an 8 day trip? I will assume the answer is "no", and that is because you would have been spending your own money and not the taxpayers.

There was a jaunt to lovely picture -postcard Italy that set us back nine grand. That is an amount that they could have made back if they bet on the right runner at the dog track, where the Environment Committee spent £1,004 as part of an inquiry into greyhound welfare.

Three MPs from the Home Affairs Committee spent £4,040 on a two day trip to Copenhagen and Malmo as part of an inquiry into prostitution.

They wanted to know if they could put it on expenses. That's not true, I made that up.

Perhaps they don't have telephones in Sweden and our MPs needed to go to take a wide-eyed peek at what was available, in person.

A six day visit to New York for three MPs on the Women and Equalities Committee cost £11,842 - that's about £4,000 each for less than a week's trip.

The Justice Committee, spent £47,413 of your money in March on just five days in New York and Boston, as part of an inquiry into young adult offenders.

I think we have just located some old adult offenders.

Of course, being a part of a select committee is not all jolly jaunts to far-off spots. The money comes in handy as well: an extra fifteen grand a year for being so kind as to chair one.

Select Committees also spent £48,000 on what they call "entertainment, seminars and other expenses".

Entertainment? Who's on the bill? Adele?

A full £328,000 was spent on producing transcripts of their meetings, if you can believe that.

A third of a million pounds on a copy machine to print up all the pronouncements of committees that amounted to nothing and were read by absolutely no-one at all.

Our MPs had better stay on their summer breaks. The country can't afford them to come back to "work".

22.08.16

Man the lifeboats

The SS Great Britain is holed under the waterline, listing heavily, heading for the rocks and the captain and all but one of her crew have abandoned ship, but don't worry because we have Petty Officer Boris at the helm.

Just when you thought it couldn't get any worse, Boris Johnson has been left in charge of the whole country while Theresa goes yomping across Switzerland with her old man and two ski poles.

Mrs M says that they are useful. Poles, she says, come in handy when you are unsure on your feet, walking over rocky terrain, or your sink needs unblocking.

It says a lot about our elected representatives that they have been going on and on about the difficult turbulent times we are living through, the economy might tank, we all might be jobless, we are looking at our imminent ruin and the moment she gets in office, our new Prime Minister is so confident about the future that she downs tools and swans off on holiday.

When was the last time you walked into a new job and said, "Right, I'm off for seven weeks, see you later"? You'd get fired that same day.

Either things aren't as bad as they are painting them, or there's not much our MPs can actually do about it.

If this is a looming catastrophe and the most perilous time we have had outside war, what with the EU withdrawal and the ongoing economic crisis, that might be overtaken by an even bigger economic crisis, perhaps the people running the country should be at their desks.

How can they possibly justify taking off all of August and half of September if this is the moment we need them most?

They will no doubt come out with some old guff about working hard in their constituencies and putting in the hours on their lap-tops abroad but they're most likely stuck in to their mini bar straight after breakfast and spending the rest of the day drifting in and out of consciousness by the pool.

The real reason none of them wants to say that it might be a good idea to skip the seven week summer holiday is that it would set a precedent.

If they stayed at the office this year, then any time there is a national calamity in the future, which on past form would be most of the time, they would be obliged to cancel their vacations.

So whatever is happening to the country, the whole thing is put on pause while they all jet off to Europe and pretend to be Irish, so as to avoid any furious questions from the locals about our EU referendum result.

Theresa has gone away to stamp through the edelweiss and left Boris Johnson at the helm.

We would have been better off with the Downing Street cats in charge. They would less likely to leave a mess on the carpet.

A spokesman assured us that the PM was still in charge, even though you'd need a cowbell and flugelhorn to reach her where she's staying.

In an emergency, we could semaphore to her from an adjacent mountain top.

Fortunately, in keeping with his pretend position as Foreign Secretary, Boris has been given no power of any kind whatsoever.

He has no appointments to meet any one important, except the milkman who needs paying at the end of the week.

He's in charge but not actually allowed to touch anything.

It's as though Theresa is punishing him by giving him what he wants - a position of power - but then taking all the power away and leaving him with just the position.

His job seems to be to catch the red-eye flight to somewhere while boning up on boxes of boring information that he needs to memorise and then apologising for some past gaffe when he gets there.

Perhaps he could spend all his free time while he is briefly running the country by playing a game of rugby with ten year olds, or how about a ride on one of those new-fangled zip wires - I hear they're LOTS of fun.

25.08.16

Busy doing nothing

What I am about to write may come as a shock. Are you sitting down? Of course you are, because despite what our haul of Olympic medals may lead you to believe, Great Britain is not a nation of super-fit sportspersons.

In the league table of fatness, we are joint gold medal winners with the USA.

You would think that the government, whose first duty is to protect the health of the nation, would want to do something about it, and they do, just as long as it does not impact on the profitably of any of their friends in the food conglomerates.

Food industry lobbyists met health ministers 40 times before the Government issued its obesity strategy, which is to cross their fingers and hope the problem goes away.

The Government stands accused of caving in to industry pressure on junk food, calories, advertising to children and sugar content.

The result will be an ever fatter country, with the young condemned to a life of wheezing bad health and a shorter time on earth than the previous generation but at least no burger or soft drinks company's big fat bottom line will suffer.

Ministers scrapped plans to ban TV adverts for unhealthy food and abandoned a proposal to get rid of cartoon characters on children's food packaging.

Don't think that those 40 meetings with the representatives of the junk food dealers had anything to do with it, though, goodness me no, whatever gave you that idea?

Jamie Oliver is so angry he has threatened to have another child and call it something stupid.

Not only did the government completely cave in on advertising and marketing junk food to children they also failed to ban dangerous trans-fats. If you do an internet search on trans fats, a picture of Edvard Munch's The Scream comes up.

The American Heart Association's website says that little was known about trans fats until 1990 when research discovered how bad they are. The government have known about this for 26 years and they still will not do anything about it. The Americans, meanwhile, have banned the ingredient.

Doctors hate trans fats but food companies love them. They are artificially created by adding hydrogen to liquid vegetable oils to make them more solid and easier to cook with and give it a longer shelf life.

They are everywhere, in fried foods like doughnuts, and baked goods like cakes, pies, biscuits, frozen pizza and margarine. If you eat ready-made food, then you are probably eating a lot of trans fats.

The problem is that these fats raise your "bad" cholesterol and lower your "good" cholesterol, increase the likelihood of developing heart disease, having a stroke and dying, but nothing so serious that the government would want to do anything about it.

They also did nothing to force companies to reduce the sugar in food.

If you require proof that the government does not care about you or your health, look no further.

According to Department of Health records, as well as the powerful Food and Drink Federation and the Advertising Association trade group, in the past two years, former public health minister Jane Ellison met representatives of Coca-Cola, KFC, Pizza Hut, Tesco, Nando's, Nestle, Kellogg's and McDonald's.

Basically, a roll call of the makers and suppliers of everything that has made us the svelte athletes that we are today.

Government officials were keen to point out that ministers had also met with dozens of health charities in that time, it's just that they didn't listen to *them*.

30.08.16

How to be popular

Mrs M has a lot on her plate. We know this when we open our morning newspaper.

If it is one of the very few that supported staying in the EU, it is full of articles saying what a calamitous state our economy is in and how it is just going to get worse.

If you buy one of the organs that wanted out of the EU, it is full of columnists telling us what a great opportunity we have in splitting from The Dark Side.

Either way, the implication is that it is all hands on deck, noses to the grindstone, sleeves rolled up and no time for lunch.

The new Drear Leader knows this and so the very first thing she did on claiming the top job was to take a vacation.

On taking the reigns of a country in turmoil, her first action was to put the reigns down again and go yomping through the edelweiss like she was courting Vince Hill.

If you are under the age of 50, I know what you are thinking. You are thinking: who is Vince Hill?

Vince Hill was a British singer of easy-listening popular music and a contemporary of Engelbert Humperdinck.

If you are still under 50, you are probably thinking: what is an Engelbert Humperdinck?

It sounds like something you need to be put in traction for, or perhaps it is a speed reduction measure on a side road in a built up area.

Both men were light entertainment stars from the era of black and white television.

If you are under the age of 20, you are probably thinking: what is an "television"?

I am sorry but I don't have all day to answer questions.

Theresa May does though. She appears to have all the time in the world.

After two weeks gambolling between schlosses, pausing to admire the views and reflect on what an easy job it is being Prime Minister, Mrs M got on the first plane home and went straight to work, by which I mean she spent the day watching cricket.

She was spotted in the VIP box, which is odd as it is not normally open to the unemployed.

The care-free PM enjoyed the free seats and the free refreshments and her free time.

This summer reverie can not last forever though, the office beckons, which is why this Wednesday she is off to her place in the country for a "brainstorming session".

Businesses often send their staff on such jaunts and their workers treat them as the break from work they have been yearning for.

Once she gets back from the holiday, and the day off for the cricket and the day away in the country, she will be fully refreshed and it will be work, work, work for ten whole days, not including weekends, and then it is back on holiday.

Parliament takes seven weeks off for the summer, gets back on the 5th September and then breaks up again less than a fortnight later for conference season.

This is an opportunity for our representatives to get away from the constraints of their families and Westminster to an all expenses paid hotel, where they will book adjoining rooms with their most youthful and eager assistants.

Three weeks of larks and hi-jinks later, the MPs return to put the country to rights. Two weeks after that they take another holiday, which prepares them for the Christmas break less than a month later.

The popularity of Theresa May is off the scale. This often happens when a new leader steps into Number 10.

This time though, the people seem to especially love their new Prime Minister. It is probably because she hasn't done anything yet.

05.09.16

Going, going, gongs.

In this week's surprisingly nimble and serious column, (considering I am wearing high heels, clown make-up and a comedian's luminous French hat) I examine two conflicting stories about our economy that should give pause to anyone who has designs on asking the public what they think of anything.

One is a survey of our nation's most expert industrialists and businesspersons that paints a gloomy picture of our economic prospects. The other is the fact that the most inexpert public have ignored those warnings and gone on a spending spree that you could see from space.

We each owe more money on credit cards than Keith Vaz spends on a night in, yet we are out there banging the plastic down like the world is having a going-out-of-business sale.

Pretty much the only thing that is propping up the British economy, apart from the banking racket, is us buying things we don't need with money we haven't got.

Fortunately, our leaders know this and have reigned in government spending. In other news, the outgoing PM David Cameron threw a £12m gift-giving party for his chums before he swanned off to spend more time with his wetsuit.

He gave his advisors, mates, donors and hairstylists a farewell money shower by raising their salaries by up to 25% and then gifted them 100% more than they were entitled to as severance pay.

He also splashed out on so many weighty gongs, titles and honours that it is surprising this island is still afloat.

Still, it's not his money, what does he care?

The good news is that while the PM went mad with the generosity while leaving power, at least lowly MPs are not still filling their boots with dodgy expenses claims because they are closely monitored by the Parliamentary Standards Authority.

The bad news is that Paul Flynn, the Shadow Leader of the House of Commons, thinks that scrutiny is irritating and that his ilk should go back to marking their own homework.

He, and others like him, believe MPs should not have to submit receipts and that they should just be given the money they say they have spent in the line of their duties, no questions asked.

That thought did not get much support because MPs were concerned about what we would think.

Well, what would the public think if we had £5m to spare, and we spend it on keeping in the country a sparkly hair grip as used by an old queen, instead of spending it on the treatment of soldiers who have come back mentally scarred from the battle field?

Queen Victoria's coronet is at risk of being spirited abroad. Isn't that awful? How will we cope?

I have no idea what a coronet is, but it is not a tiara, and it definitely is not a crown and it absolutely must not leave the country, so unless there is a generous member of the public who would like to pay £5m for a shiny hair thing and give it back to the royal family, then the public will be paying for it.

What would the public think about that?

It might be best not to ask, the public have a tendency to surprise.

They certainly did when ITV shut down their most popular television station for an hour to entice its viewers to go outside to catch some of that Olympics fever and move about a bit.

A full 60,000 of them decided to stay right where they were, looking at a blank screen until Philip Schofield reappeared.

06.09.16

Time to trust again?

Just when you though that the Labour Party could not get any less electable, along came Paul Flynn, the Shadow Leader of the House of Commons, Shadow Secretary of State for Wales and Labour's expenses spokesperson.

That sounds like a full plate. Should he need another job, he could be Jeremy Corbyn's stunt double, and he is the possessor of a beard that would make him an ideal toilet brush.

Mr Flynn said that we should forget what happened in the past with MP's expenses and from this moment on we should just give them whatever money they say they have spent and trust them to be honest.

No one in this country has trusted their MP to be honest since the Daily Telegraph acquired the details of their expenses and started to publish them in 2009.

We weren't too sure about them before that either.

Paul Flynn said that because the current procedure is a time consuming chore, Parliamentary expenses should be scrapped and MPs trusted with an allowance.

He said that MPs resent having to submit expenses claims because it takes too long and that the parliamentary watchdog should be scrapped and MPs sent automatic payments without having to submit expense claims, leaving them more time to shop for duck houses.

I made that last part up.

What is strange is that Flynn's suggestions have gained credence with the same newspaper that dumped them in the mire.

The paper published a lengthy column by the ex- Labour MP and current journalist Tom Harris who agreed with Flynn's central tenet that the current system is unworkable, time consuming, inefficient and broken.

Harris says that Paul Flynn is right and that all MPs should get a generous allowance on top of their salary, no questions asked. He said that it will not happen, however, because the public won't go for it.

You bet we won't. If Theresa May put her considerable weight behind such a proposal we would think that the hairspray fumes had gone to her brain.

Just the very idea of letting our members of parliament run free with more of our money makes the public's eyes revolve into the backs of their heads and foam start coming out of their ears.

The problem is, it might be the right thing to do. If the Independent Parliamentary Standards Authority is wasting time and money in chasing every invoice for a paper clip or second class stamp, then it is to our detriment.

We need someone with a truly spotless reputation to put the case for change.

Unfortunately, when the Telegraph scoured the information it had received in 2009, it discovered that Paul Flynn charged us over £8,000 for a new kitchen and carpets and twelve hundred pounds worth of decoration to his flat before he sold it for a tidy return and moved to another one. We paid to tart it up, he trousered the profit.

He had to repay more than £2,600 in mortgage interest.

His was not the most egregious case of being casual with the public's money but he is not the unsullied innocent that could persuade us to loosen the purse strings either.

Westminster will echo to the sound of invoices being stapled to expenses forms for a while yet.

12.09.16

The tax man's little secret

The EU are taking the tech giant Apple to task because when the European Parliament transferred their iTunes albums from one computer to another, they did not end up with 3000 perfectly curated and ordered albums, they found they had 3000 tracks marked '1" and 3000 tracks marked "2" and so on.

There was no indication what those tracks were and no way of putting them in the right order. You can imagine how furious the EU were, especially when they had followed Apple's instructions on transferring the files to the letter.

Oh wait...that wasn't the EU, that was me.

What the EU are furious about is that Apple apparently pay tax at a rate which is so small you would need a magnifying glass to see it.

If you paid tax at the same rate that Apple are accused of paying, on a salary of £30,000 a year, your tax bill would be £1.

I will assume that your head has just exploded.

We would expect that giant corporations with no fixed abode could pit one country against another and find a way to claim they are resident for tax purposes on a planet in a far off galaxy, billions of light years away.

What we might not expect is that we could reduce our tax bill by millions of pounds over our lifetime by letting a member of the public walk across our garden once a year.

The Defence Minister and Deputy Leader of the House of Lords, Lord Howe, struck a confidential deal with the taxman when he inherited his country estate, all 1,550 acres of it.

You did not reach a confidential deal with the tax man when you inherited from your parents, because you only inherited an old suitcase and a receding hairline.

Lord Howe secured a great little deal with Her Majesty's Revenue and Customs that meant he did not have to pay the full tax due on the inheritance of his £30m estate because of what they call a Conditional Exemption Agreement.

It is the sort of thing that the very rich use in order to avoid paying what could have been millions of pounds in tax, that could have funded operations to save the sight of those going blind, or fixed the pothole in the road that the blind might fall into.

Did you know that you can traipse across Lord Howe's lawns and fields and carpets too?

Well, you can because the Conditional Exemption Agreement means that for overlooking the tax that would ordinarily have been paid on the inheritance of a £30m estate, we the public are allowed access to the grounds and the historic house on it.

This is all completely open and transparent, except for the parts that are totally secret and opaque.

Lord Howe got tax relief on the value of 70 works of art because the public would be allowed to see them by making an appointment.

They are works of art like paintings and dining chairs. You can't get such a deal because you got your dining chairs from Ikea and no one wants to see your picture of a clown crying.

HMRC agreed to reduce the tax bill of one of the richest people in the land because you and I could book a tour of his living room, assuming we had heard of him, knew about the deal and could attend on the two days in the year when the offer is available.

There are about 340 buildings and areas of land that have a deal in place like this. The landed gentry get to swerve the tax that you and I would have to pay because they can get a one-on-one meeting with the tax man who seems disposed to let them keep their money on the spurious grounds that we can go and gawp at their stuff for a few minutes a year.

Do not try this yourself. You will go to jail if you try to tell the tax man that you will not pay any tax this year because you have invited your neighbour round for a shufti at your nicknacks.

The authorities bang on about these kind of deals being for the preservation of heritage assets but it looks more like they are about the preservation of the wealth and power of the establishment.

If they were confident of their position, all this would in the open, but such deals are covered by more veils than a Moroccan belly dancer.

The owners of these places don't want the public to know about these deals because they might have hordes of scrofulous riff-raff fingering their credenzas.

The government certainly do not want about us to know about them because they will make us angry and we might just be woken from our Dancing With The X-factor On Ice slumber and might take to the battlements and demand a tax cut for ourselves.

20.09.16

Advanced driving manoeuvres.

Traffic update: beware the woman who does not want to go to New Jersey.

If you have ever been to New Jersey, or have seen The Sopranos, you will understand the lady who panicked in front of the Lincoln Tunnel in New York that connects Manhattan to the place whose official state shell is the knobbled whelk. I am not making that up.

The state slogan of New Jersey is "come and see for yourself". This woman did not want to do that.

On driving through mid-town Manhattan, she found herself in one-way traffic heading towards the Lincoln Tunnel that goes under the Hudson River and emerges in the place whose state dinosaur is Jon Bon Jovi.

Just kidding, the official state dinosaur of New Jersey is the Hadrosaurus, from the Greek "hadros" meaning bulky and "saurus" meaning lizard. It is the state of the bulky lizard, also known as New Jersey Governor Chris Christie.

If you have ever accidentally found yourself approaching the Blackwall Tunnel in London, you will understand this woman's response, which was to stop dead in the middle of the road, causing a jam which stretched to the moon and back.

She explained to a quizzical policeperson that she did not want to go to Jersey and he related the news that as she was in a one-way traffic system, she had no choice, but where there is a will, there is a way.

Her way was to turn her car around and start driving into oncoming traffic as though she was in one of those Jason Bourne films. The police tried to stop her and one was hit for his trouble.

She was successfully apprehended some while later, after running a red light, and was charged with assault, unlawful fleeing and breaking a whole host of other traffic laws, some of which had to be invented just for her.

Meanwhile, in Austria a couple were driving through the picturesque north-west of the country, somewhat naked from the waist down.

They were "enjoying themselves" when a deer stepped out into the road and the male driver was forced to brake the car violently, which in turn caused his lady friend to accidentally bite down on his personal area.

An ambulance rushed to the scene after a frantic call reporting a tooth related intimate injury following a car crash, which must have been a first for Austria, but which is probably routine in New Jersey.

The local paper, which is called The Local, assured its readers that any damage was superficial and he should be back in working order by the time you read this.

The moral of these two stories is the same: take the bus.

26.09.16

Money up in smoke

In November, when America will go to the polls to decide on who wins the Comedy Clown Race to the Whitehouse, some will also vote on whether marijuana should be legalised in their state.

Americans may need all the drugs the can lay their hands on to mitigate the shock of who their next leader will be.

One such state is California, which is allowing its citizens to vote on legalising the recreational use of marijuana.

They already allow its use for medical reasons.

From what I am told, acquiring a prescription for medical marijuana in the US is just a matter of paying for a GP visit to complain about tension, or headaches or a family history of glaucoma or you have a Pink Floyd album you want to listen to and will go to another doctor if they don't give you what you want.

Colorado, Washington, Alaska, and Oregon already allow the sale and possession of marijuana for both medical and recreational use.

Twenty-three states and the District of Columbia have passed laws allowing some degree of medical use of marijuana, and 14 states have taken steps to decriminalize it.

According to the Arcview Group, an American cannabis investment and research firm, medical and recreational marijuana sales are expected to more than double to $6.5billion in California alone by 2020 if the drug becomes fully legal after November, which it is expected to do.

Arizona, Maine, Massachusetts and Nevada will also vote on legalizing recreational marijuana on November 8

The amount of money that will be made, and the taxes paid on it are huge.

Colorado earns about $100m a year in tax on the sale of marijuana and there are only 5 million people in Colorado.

America has a population of about 320m people, so if the rest of the country consumes it the way Colorado does, then it is potentially worth billions dollars in tax revenue that would otherwise go straight into the pockets of criminals, who will use it to buy guns to safeguard their businesses.

In Great Britain, there has been yet more studies that say we should allow it to be fully or partly legalised.

According to a new major inquiry by MPs and peers, cannabis should be legalised in the UK for medical use,

A report by the All-Party Parliamentary Group on Drug Reform has concluded that the current refusal to recognise the medical value of cannabis is "irrational", and called for an end to the criminalisation of hundreds of thousands of people who use the drug to relieve pain.

In March, another British study said legalising the sale of cannabis in specialist shops could raise £1billion in tax revenues while reducing the harm done to users.

A panel of experts including scientists, academics and police bosses concluded that the UK should follow some US states in allowing over 18s to purchase cannabis in licensed stores.

They were people like Former Liberal Democrat health minister Norman Lamb, Mike Barton, the Chief Constable of Durham Constabulary, Niamh Eastwood, executive director of the drugs charity Release and Professor David Nutt, the former chair of the Advisory Committee on the Misuse of Drugs.

Yes, that Nutt! When he was the government's drugs czar, it was just too easy for the press to dismiss the opinions of a man with that surname. Fish in a barrel.

In the report they said: "Drug policy to date has (almost) always been driven by political and ideological agendas that have ignored scientific, public health and social policy norms."

Faced with this fresh charge that successive prime ministers have ignored scientific, public health and social policy norms, the current PM will doubtless act to type, bat this aside and carry on regardless.

As you may have heard. the government is not interested in experts and their so-called facts.

30.09.16

The red woman, orange man show

After the debate, Donald Trump announced that he won and the moderator lost and the person who put the microphone on him lost, and the mainstream media lost and Chris Rea's favourite -The Woman In Red - lost big time.

She lost tremendously bigly...huge, or as he would say: yoooge.

Down here on earth, Hillary won the debate by 62% to 27% according to a CNN poll.

That means 11% of the people thought that neither candidate won, or they were watching the background scenery and weren't paying attention, or they were so dazzled by Hillary's bright red storm-trooper outfit that they couldn't see where to write their opinion.

Other polls went the other way, the internet polls were for Trump, the professional polls favoured Clinton but a most interesting one said that for 80%, the debate had not changed their minds one way or the other.

When they came on stage, the first question of the evening was: what colour is Donald Trump today?

He normally makes you reach for the remote to fiddle with the settings.

He makes you think your TV is on the fritz because he usually looks orange, like a fruit basket.

For the debate, though, someone had toned his face down to a peach powder blush

He still looked like someone had shaved the back of a ginger cat but it was an improvement.

Hilary on the other hand was all dressed up in Republican red and looked animatronic, like one of those robots that welcome you to the kiddies' rides at Disneyworld.

Meanwhile, Donald was sniffing and sniffing and taking sips of water and afterwards blamed the microphone, saying that he wasn't sniffing, there was something wrong with his mike.

Howard Dean, the former Governor of Vermont, ex-Chairman of the Democratic National Committee and once a doctor, tweeted during the debate that Donald Trump has a cocaine problem and that is why he was sniffing.

He said it would also explain his erratic behaviour. Dean went on MSNBC the next day and far from rowing back from his accusation, he repeated it. Oddly, no-one from Trump's camp complained about it at all. No denials, no outrage, nothing.

As for what they said - well, Trump said that he will stop American jobs going overseas, but this is a man who has a lot of product lines, all with his name on naturally. Few are made in the USA.

He has Donald Trump shirts made in Korea, Donald Trump suits made in Indonesia, Donald Trump eyeglasses made in China, Donald Trump furniture made in Germany, Donald Trump mirrors made in China, Donald Trump picture frames made in India, and Donald Trump vodka made in the Netherlands, not to mention all the things he gets made in Mexico, the country he berates the most

Hilary didn't mention any of that at all.

When it got to tax, Trump said he wants to reduce corporation tax by over half to 15% and said he earned $694m last year and appeared to boast that he paid no tax on that, because he is "smart".

You would think that would hurt his support among everyone not in the the top 1%.

That he said that as though it was a positive attribute shows how completely disconnected from most people's thinking he is.

Among his billionaire friends, you would assume that they would joke about such things and congratulate themselves on their ability to avoid taxes but you would not think it would go down too well with the rest of the population, who have to pay their taxes to make up the shortfall caused by those that do not.

Oddly, Hilary didn't make much of that either.

Maybe she was concentrating too hard on keeping her eyes from swivelling in opposite directions.

She also didn't call him out on his claim that he got a "small" loan from his father to start his business - it was $14m by his own admission and others have estimated it as anything up to $300m from his father's estate.

Even if it was $14m as Donald said - to describe that as a small loan is not very relatable to the people he is asking to support him.

He also dismissed the accusation that he doesn't pay the ordinary hard working types he gets to do jobs for him.

There are literally thousands of people that have complained that they did work for him and then he refused to pay them.

When Hilary claimed that during the property slump and the financial crash that Trump said he hoped the property market would tank because he could buy property on the cheap - profiting from the misery of others - he just said that is good business.

He is a man who doesn't pay his bills, who doesn't pay taxes, who profits from the misfortune of others, has taken American jobs and shipped them overseas and wants tax cuts for himself and the rich.

You would think all that would be knock out blows for his chances of getting into the Whitehouse.

Yet it didn't look to me that Hilary really won the night, partly because Trump was much more aggressive than her, dominated the speaking and when the spotlight fell away from him, simply shouted louder to drown her and the moderator out.

He also has this mesmerising way with waving his hands about, which as you've seen on television is the current default way of keeping attention and emphasising a point.

Look at any old documentary from the 1970s, say, and the first thing you notice, apart from the absence of background music, is that the person speaking to camera has their arms by their sides. Attention spans were longer then.

These days, everyone from news reporters to wild life presenters have been told to wave their arms about like they are directing traffic, because it keeps the attention of people who can't concentrate.

Trump appeared to be a bully and aggressive and quick to anger and to some people they like that - they want a strong man, like President Putin.

Put your faith in the tough guy and he will sort things out for you.

For the rest of us, it is a bit alarming that a big shouty man-baby, so easily riled and unconcerned about others could become the next President of the United States of America

It would be like making the school bully the headmaster - what could possibly go wrong?

The national polls are still neck and neck, it is all to play for, and on October 9th it will be seconds out, round two.

07.10.16

Image Problem? Get A Bunny.

The Tories are in such a flap to change the public's perception of them as the nasty party that they are flailing around like a squid that wants a cuddle.

The Chancellor, Philip Hammond, has hit out at big businesses for 'angering their customers' by not addressing issues such as workers' rights and executive pay.

Does he mean banks? They are the biggest criminals when it comes to executive pay and yet, even though it is easy and can be done in 7 days, only about a million of us a year switch our bank accounts.

That sounds a lot until you know that there are 46m current accounts open in the UK and we stay with our banks, no matter what they do, for an average of 17 years, which is 6 years longer than most people stay with their partners, and we get to have sex with our partners!

Philip Hammond is wrong. We are not remotely angry with companies that don't treat their staff well and use their profits to fill their executives' swimming pools with cash.

Are we boycotting the tech companies that not only don't pay taxes but get their shiny things made in sweat shops in the Far East that are so bad for their workers, that suicide seems like a better option than coming to work?

We couldn't care less about those workers' rights. We ignore their pain and form an orderly queue the next time they release some new thinner, larger, more shiny and curvy phone.

We care about as much for workers' rights as we care about the welfare of the animals we eat or that squeeze out eggs for us.

If we cared, we would buy ethically produced, organic, free trade, pollution neutral, workers' co-op goods, but we think that people that do that are hippies at best and Jeremy Corbyn at worst.

People that care about the environment and workers' rights are derided as kooks, dangerous radicals, socialists and 60's throwbacks.

It was such an odd thing for a Conservative minister to say. Perhaps he is a caring and thoroughly modern chancellor, but I wouldn't bet on it.

I don't want to come over like a nutcase conspiracy theorist, but it makes me wonder whether he is saying that to make it appear that the Conservative government cares, to step on Labour's territory and negate any surge in popularity for Jeremy Corbyn, because if the people just read what Jezza is proposing, they might find that they agree with him quite a lot.

Philip Hammond said 'Business needs to understand it isn't sustainable to have large household brand-name businesses angering their consumers,'

But customers don't change their behaviour based on how big brands treat their staff and executives.

He said it is important that firms see how consumers view them and their image.

Well, what is the image of the burger place on the high street? What is the image of the tax dodging phone manufacturer, what is the image of the polluting oil company, the rip off bank?

They are all doing fabulously well despite having terrible images because we do not care that they all engage in terrible behaviour.

Our opinion of a company is not rooted in what they do, it is based on the number of cute cartoon bunnies they have in their television advertising.

10.10.16

The squib that fizzled.

If ever a fight did not live up to it's hype, it was this one.

The build-up was extraordinary. The Donald sought to take charge of the accusations of misogyny that had been levelled at him all week by holding an extraordinary and unexpected press conference with four women who presumably had a tale to tell of their treatment at the hands of Bill Clinton.

Trump announced them one by one, apart from the lady on the end whose name he had presumably forgotten. Apart from one room-silencing allegation of rape, the others failed to fully explain why they were there. Perhaps the American audience is already familiar with their stories.

The pre-publicity pegged this as the battle of the century, an epic Rock 'em Sock 'em, paint the walls with blood, drag out the carcass of the loser, bare knuckle smack down.

What we got was more of the same with better hair and clothes. The hair was courtesy of a glamour-puss moderator called Anderson Cooper, whose steely, precision-crafted, luminous white barnet was so bright it could be used to signal to life on other planets.

The better dressed was Hillary. In the previous debate, she looked like she was auditioning for the role of lead baton twirler in a Disney Parade. This time, she sported a much more toned down look that was not so hard to gaze at without sunglasses. She was perfectly presented like she had just come out of a box.

Donald shuffled on like a family fridge had been cloaked in a suit that had been left in the garden overnight. His tie hung down to about where his knees must be, it is hard to tell because he does not seem to bend them.

It was a giant red arrow pointing to the area he would like us to think that his Donaldhood ends.

There was no microphone malfunction this time. The contestants hand-held their mikes, so the sound they made was all of their own doing.

Hilary made that whiny nasal noise that Bill has had to get used to, Donald wheezed and sniffed and gasped for breath like a dirty phone call.

His nose appears to have been squashed so much that air can't get through. Maybe Robert De Nero had punched him in the face.

The first question was of the "locker room" sex banter that dominated the media this week, despite having been recorded over ten years ago. Was Trump aware that he had bragged that he sexually assaulted women?

Donald's frown deepened to a depth to which submarines can't dive. He explained that, no of course he did not, it was all a mistake, that didn't happen and if it did he was very sorry, he apologises, it is not who he is, no-one has more respect for women than he, his respect for women is tremendously tremendous.

Hilary politely disagreed but did not hang on the topic so much that her husband's shenanigans might come to dominate the proceedings.

Trump got applause for saying Hilary should be ashamed for concentrating on something that happened ten years ago, and then proceeded to criticise her for things that she had done ten years ago.

He glowered and roamed the stage like an ageing boxer, gripped the back of the stool he didn't sit on, and scrapped with Hilary and both moderators simultaneously.

He could pick a fight in solitary confinement.

They weren't giving him enough time, they did not interrupt Hilary like they did him, it was three against one...the sort of whiny school-boy complaining that might get him a better deal in a business negotiation but was not very attractive in high definition in peoples' living rooms.

Hilary, meanwhile, perched attentively on her stool when listening, and ran through the whole gamut of the polished professional politician.

She addressed the audience questioners by name, gave her answers to their face and smiled without pause. Her facial muscles must be strong enough to pick up a car battery.

The night was light on detail, policy, plans and direction.

Those that had already made up their minds will probably not have changed their voting intentions. There was no great snafu, nothing that would drop a jaw in a ten second clip on YouTube.

The last question was the best of the night. Was there anything about the other candidate that they admired?

Trump was asked to go first but Hillary jumped in, giving Donald time to think. She could not bring herself to admire anything about her opposite number except his children. If in doubt, praise the kids.

Trump pulled a rabbit out of the hat by appearing the more magnanimous at the last by crediting her as a fighter who does not give up.

Who knew he could be so presidential?

20.10.16

All White On The Night.

Now we know where Hilary has been all week. She died. The white ghost of Mrs Clinton floated onto the stage in Las Vegas - white hair, white teeth, white suit, like the medical purser of a cruise ship lost at sea in the late 1800's.

Her hairstyle looked to have cost as much as her opponent had spent on his suit. That is not a slight on his tailor.

The American flag pinned to his lapel, power tie predominant, the one-man maelstrom that is Donald Trump moved to grip his podium as though he was engaging it in a wrestling bout.

Hand shakes there were none.

For this debate The Donald had selected a colour for his face that human beings often come in. Gone was that dusky peach shade of a 1970's bathroom suite.

Absent also was his crowd-pleasing showmanship. This was a toned down Donald that was prepared to engage with the issues. Considering the crushing pressure he is under, he did very well.

Speaking substantively is not his metier. He has got this far by being a grandiose, blustering stand -up comic of a candidate. His popularity propelled as much by what he says as how he says it.

In the final debate of the Comedy Clown Race To The White House, almost all of the funny had been excised from his act. It was the night that the race got serious.

He appealed to the gun lovers and the abortion haters and you could sense the right-wing pulling their chairs closer to the screen.

He spoke of mass immigration and the loss of jobs and his answers were at least the equal of Hillary's for much of the night.

He actually appeared to be winning for a good part of the debate. Even the sniff had been conquered.

His demeanour was the antithesis of his past performances - more softly spoken and less interrupty.

For the most part, Trump was actually calmer than Hilary, who seemed angrier and more forceful of late. Perhaps she can not believe that she still has not conclusively buried the chances of a game show host off the telly becoming the successor to Oback Arama.

It could be something about the sound they both make when speaking. Trump is sonorous and yet sing-song in his delivery. His dancing hands are mesmerising.

Clinton, on the other hand, has a monotone, droning, somnambulistic quality to her voice.

The only thing on her that moves is her mouth. Everything else about her face and body is static as though frozen in aspic.

Whether she appeared presidential is questionable. He certainly did. If you knew nothing about either candidate and saw them for the very first time you would pick Trump as the person with the top job.

That might have something to do with the traditional roles of the sexes.

These things matter. In times of great danger, like war, people are drawn to strong figures that appear to offer protection. You wouldn't want to be in a fist fight against Trump with only Hillary by your side.

Overall, there was no knock-out punch landed. Hillary won on women's issues, like abortion, Trump won on masculine concerns like guns and defence.

The post-debate polls released on the 20th October showed that the needle had moved towards the Republican candidate.

The LA Times have them in a tie at 44% each, Trump is showing a 1% lead in the Investor's Business Daily IBD/TIPP survey when the two other main candidates are included (yes, there are other candidates) and Rasmussen has Trump ahead by 3%.

Those are the figures representing the popular vote but that is not what wins the race for the Whitehouse, as Al Gore knows. He won the most votes in 2000 but still lost to George W Bush after the debacle of the Hanging Chads Of Florida.

The headline of the night was Trump's refusal to say that he would accept the result.

The Democrats were furious, forgetting the concession that their candidate Al Gore made in 2000, swiftly followed by his rescinding of that concession when he thought that he might win because Floridians had been too frail to punch a hole in a piece of paper.

Bush sued, the courts stopped the recount after what seemed an eternity and W won.

Who could confidently predict what will happen in the next three weeks?

Isn't it exciting?

24.10.16

It's not just national security - it's bigger than that.

A massive co-ordinated series of cyber attacks forced hundreds of major websites including Amazon and Twitter offline last Sunday.

Some people are saying that the security breach could be practice for disrupting the US election.

Those people might just be journalists making stories up to fill the gaps in their newspapers between items on women Donald Trump is accused of squeezing and the body count in Emmerdale.

WikiLeaks believes its supporters were responsible and urged them to 'stop taking down the US internet'.

It is nice of WikiLeaks to say that but also alarming that something that is so fundamental to modern life can be obliterated by a disaffected teen on his lap-top.

Of course, it could have been the Russians attempting to subvert democracy.

The belief is that the Kremlin has been trying to shoe-horn The Donald into the Whitehouse as they believe Trump is sensitive to Russia's desires, whereas Hillary might require a big cheque to come onside, and since the fall in the price of oil, Russia is fresh out of money and couldn't come up with anything like the amount that Clinton is used to receiving for making a formal address. They couldn't afford a thumbs up.

The Ecuadoreans switched off Julian Assange's internet service in its UK embassy after he released another tranche of emails showing the contents of a speech given by Hillary Clinton to Goldman Sachs who certainly do have the resources to get Hillary at one of their shindigs.

It has been suggested that the Ecuadoreans were pressured into removing Julian Assange's access to the world wide web by the Americans. The US have claimed their innocence, and if you believe that, I have a rare upside down £5 note I would like to sell you.

When the internet was taken down, Wikileaks tweeted: 'The Obama administration should not have attempted to misuse its instruments of state to stop criticism of its ruling party candidate.'

They are citing political interference as the reason for the attack that left a great deal of the United States communicating with each other like it was 1989.

Concerns about the security of the web and of the attack on freedom of speech aside, it is worrying that a few eager computer nerds can take out the internet feed for much of the richest country on earth.

Pretty much everything we now do is controlled online. When Amazon and Twitter went dark it meant that people could not Tweet how happy they were with the useless thing they just bought online.

They couldn't share pictures of them unwrapping their purchase and post videos of them rating it.

It denied users the opportunity of commenting on those posts and telling the person responsible that they are either The Greatest Thing In The Whole World Ever and deserve a heart-shaped emoticon, or they are ugly and stupid and should kill themselves.

An internet outage is bad because for a lot of people, if it is not on the internet, it does not exist.

We should count ourselves lucky. It could have been much worse.

Can you imagine your internet banking going down, or our transport network?

Without the net, people might not have been able to steal music or download The Game Of Thrones without paying for it.

If the internet went down, we could not pass the hours we are supposed to be working by looking at holiday destinations we can't afford to go to, or inside houses we don't have the money to buy.

Without the net, celebrities would not have an outlet to post their thought.

Pussycats doing cute things would be doing so only for their owners, and not for the millions who like to waste their time watching other people's pets.

Good grief, if the internet did not work, we would have to go back to buying pornography in the form of shrink-wrapped magazines, or finding torn copies of them littering railway sidings.

There is comfort in nostalgia, but no-one wants to go back to THOSE good old days.

28.10.16

It's not just Marmite, it's Bisto too.

Unilever said it and Tesco said it and Nestle said it: prices are going to go up. Tesco is the biggest retailer in the land, Unilever and Nestle are two of the biggest food companies on Earth.

These companies are packed with experts in possession of facts but we are no longer interested in experts and facts.

The lunatic wing of the Brexit Headbangers Club have declared that anyone suggesting a possible negative consequence of leaving the EU is a traitor and should have their living privileges removed, along with their heads.

We can all say we were there during Marmitegate. It was a small testing of the waters by the company Unilever which announced an across the board 10% price increase for its products supplied to Tesco.

That the press concentrated on Marmite is interesting because it is one of those Ye Olde English consumables, like HP Sauce and Birds Eye Fish Fingers that are especially loved by Kippers.

Those are brands that speak of proper Mary Poppin's prams and cricket on the green and Jackanory, before every children's television presenter stopped being an eccentric and started to become a suspect.

Marmite is the taste of Britain in black and white.

Unilever make far more than that unctuous tar, though. They also make Ben and Jerry's and Hellmann's and the food advertised to shed the weight gained by eating those products: SlimFast.

The little battle between Unilever and Tesco was settled amicably, or so we are led to believe, but despite having no knowledge of what transpired, the press called it a victory for Britain and hailed Tesco as the champion of the little people.

That can not be the same Tesco whose three former directors were charged with fraud over a £ 263m accounting scandal, nor could it be the same retailer that according to the Grocery Code Adjudicator "knowingly delayed paying money to suppliers in order to improve its own financial position", sometimes not paying a debt for two years.

Tesco are not on the side of the little people any more than Apple are a firm run by caring hippies or BP are friends to the environment.

They are aggressive capitalists out to maximise their profits. They also have a very low level of profit on everything they sell. They got so big by selling a lot at a small mark-up. If they sell even a little bit less they are in trouble.

Food companies have a much greater profit margin on what they sell and it is rather easier to avoid supermarkets that annoy their customers than it is to avoid food conglomerates.

The hundreds of house-hold brands that Unilever produce are as nothing compared to the wares that Nestle has on offer.

I could list them all here but there isn't enough room on the internet.

Pretty much everything in your kitchen and in your cat was made by ten companies.

If you don't like the price hike on one product, the chances are that the alternative you choose will have been made by the same people.

So, when two of the biggest food giants in the world, and our dominant retailer, all say that prices are going to rise because of Brexit, it might be wise to at least prepare ourselves for that eventuality and accept our decision has repercussions, rather than waving the Union flag about and shouting at the problem, expecting it to go away.

10.11.16

The Un-Invention Of Sex.

For the purpose of living happily ever after, two people used to be selected for each other by their wiser elders.

This did not work very well for those stuck with a partner that looked like the back end of a moose.

Another bad idea was the practice of saving yourself until you were married, because how can you know if you are compatible bashing your bits together, unless you try before you buy?

These days, young people would laugh at such practices, and old people would laugh right back, because what the youth are getting up to now is even more bizarre.

The night-time economy grew to provide a forum for the playing out of sex games.

Teens and twenty-somethings would go out on the pull, starting with a bucket of libation at a bar and then onto a club where they would gyrate themselves into an assignation with some young lovely that might come to fruition in one of their homes, or on the night-bus heading there, if they just could not wait one more minute.

Even in this scenario, some conversation would take place, a common ground would be identified and at least part of the decision that this was the person you wanted to be with for the rest of your life, or the rest of your night, would be made on the basis of their personality, not just on how good they looked in jeans.

Today, that is all gone, replaced by the swipe. If you have been living in a jungle retreat for the past five years, or you are over 60 years old, let me explain.

The phones that people carry round with them, the ones they stare into all day while walking into traffic, are now sex finder machines.

There are applications on them that cater for those that want to share intimate photographs of themselves with others. Fortunately, the youth of today are richly endowed with pictures of themselves.

They take more selfies than they have hot dinners, mostly because eating makes you puffy and the phone camera adds 10 pounds as it is.

Having uploaded a snap of yourself, others can then view, rate, discard, save, send a frowny face emoticon, swipe on to the next one or respond in kind. Two clicks later and you could be having wordless sex with someone whose name you do not know.

If you think that sounds impersonal, prepare yourself - it has just got worse.

Men are now cutting out the human element altogether and having a relationship with their phone, rather than using it to find a relationship with another person.

Teenagers, and others old enough to know better, are developing feelings for female and male-voiced digital assistants that come installed on their mobiles.

Ilya Eckstein, the chief executive of Robin Labs, a company that makes software that enables users to have a conversation with a computer, said his company's virtual assistant was used by some men for up to 300 conversations a day.

They are not talking about the weather.

He told The Times "As well as the people who want to talk dirty, there are men who want a deeper sort of relationship or companionship."

He said people "want to flirt, they want to dream about a subservient girlfriend, or even a sexual slave".

This is not what was envisaged by the pioneers of virtual assistants, such as the Phone's Siri and Microsoft's Cortana.

They were designed to be used for asking your device to call your mummy, or to find the nearest Pizza Express. They were not made for lonely hearts to whisper sweet disgustings to a slavebot.

A writer for Microsoft's digital assistant Cortana, said that "a good chunk of the volume of early-on inquiries" were about the chatbot's sex life.

Here is spoiler alert: chatbots do not have a sex life. They do not even have bots.

We are at the precipice of another sexual revolution. Pretty soon the technology will cut out the middle men - us.

Chatbots will be talking dirty to each other, so we don't have to.

While you sleep, your digital assistant will make lewd comments to someone else's digital assistant about wanting to have its nodes cleaned, thereby potentially removing us from the equation entirely.

If our phones ever learn to take pictures of themselves, we're sunk.

08.11.16

The Prime Minister is appealing.

Great Britain is hosting its own political comedy clownmageddon, because we do not want to be left behind in the world-wide race to the bottom of the sanity barrel.

The Director of Public Prosecutions, Alison Saunders, is investigating whether the assertions, fantasies, fables and bus signs made by the three Brexiteers and their cohorts amounted to "undue influence" in the run up to the referendum on the EU.

A complaint has been made by Professor Bob Watt, an expert in electoral law from the University of Birmingham.

Perhaps Professor Bob did not get the memo: this country has had its fill of so-called experts and their so-called facts (see M. Gove for full details).

Professor Bob is concerned that the £350m figure that the Brexiteers said the EU is costing us was not true, nor was the assertion that Turkey was about to join and that every Turk that could put one foot in front of the other was preparing to make the crossing in whatever floatation device was at hand, to land at Dover to demand their unemployment benefits and their choice of local virgins.

He may have a point, but he doesn't have a case. Almost the whole country knew that those two things were made up and the people that did not know them to be false probably also did not know that there was a referendum to vote on, or where the EU was, or how to pronounce it.

The people that voted out, did so because they wanted the rule of law to be written by the British, for the British. They also wanted to re-assert the primacy of the British Parliament and of British courts.

You would think that they, and the right-wing press that whipped their readers into such a frenzy, would be delighted at the ruling by the three High Court judges that stated that the British Parliament should be allowed its say on the direction of the British nation.

If you do think that, then you would be wrong. You would be so wrong that I would doubt that you are British or that you had ever met a British person, or read a British newspaper.

The Daily Mail, in particular, had a cow. That three of the highest legal authorities in the land should do something so democratic as to invite Parliament to have an input into the running of the country made the veins on the Mail's forehead bulge and the blood vessels in its eyes burst.

It sought to impugn the character of the judges and went directly to type by outing one as openly gay.

Things have moved on since The Mail last checked its watch in 1955. The outing of a gay judge is not really news if he is already out, so they added that he is also an ex-fencer and Olympian, as though that was tantamount to goat fondling.

The other two judges stand accused of taking government money for their professional advice and of creating a European law group...in Europe!

The headlines ran the whole gamut from "Traitors!", to "Hang 'Em All".

I made those headlines up and added the quotation marks for spurious authenticity, but obfuscation seems to be the order of the day, so why not?

I know what you're thinking...who the hell do these bewigged nonentities think they are and just what the hell is the High Court when it is at home?

Well, it is the judicial body that has, in one way or another, been running the law of this great land for five centuries, and in its current form for about 150 years.

It is the stand-in for a written constitution in this country and it is our protector such that everyone is subject to the rule of law, whereby every person no matter who they are must obey it. There is no leniency for a person because of their peerage, sex, religion or financial standing.

That is the theory anyway. The law applies to everyone, even if you are an eager Prime Minister, keen to get on with trying to fashion a victory out of the enormous turd sandwich that your predecessor gifted you.

In their demented reaction to a very simple verdict, the papers and the people that rely on them for forming their opinions, might have missed the point that the ruling was not to stop Brexit, it was just a point of law that you can not rescind an Act of Parliament by use of the Royal Prerogative. Only Parliament can do that.

The Royal Prerogative is the method by which the Queen can throw out or have changed any proposed law that she does not like the look of.

She has done this many times before, to almost no coverage in the papers whatsoever. It is as though her very real power to shape our laws is a secret.

Some of the laws she has objected to have been ones that might impact on her income. That is the way with British democracy - we can have our say but not where it might inconvenience our unelected Head of State.

The Queen can not cancel an Act of Parliament that already exists. Nor can her Prime Minister do that in the Queen's name.

The little thing that stopped that was the English Civil War. It was in all the papers. You would have thought Mrs M would have heard of it.

The three High Court judges - Larry, Curly and Moe - know of that skirmish and their ruling was simple confirmation of a principle that has been in place for about 400 years.

That Mother Theresa, nor her phalanx of hangers on, advisors, shoe polishers and lickspittles, did not know that is a little scary.

Theresa May is appealing. Oh yes she is - to the Supreme Court.

Some of her fellow Brexiteers are suggesting that she hold a snap election, making the triggering of Article 50 (the starting gun on the process of leaving the EU) an election pledge.

If she won, the thinking goes, her MPs would never vote against it because it was a solemn election promise.

This would be bound to work, because as you know, no manifesto pledge has ever been broken before in the entire history of the Mother of all Parliaments.

We should all be thanking Donald Trump for his efforts to become the next President of the United States of America. Without him, the world would all be laughing at *us*.

11.11.16

Biff Goes To Washington

Well, that didn't take long. The Republicans who had fought against Donald Trump as being a candidate too far, a loose cannon, a small handed vulgarian, irreligious, morally bankrupt and not a real Republican, have rallied to the cause, shaken his hand, promised their support and asked for a job.

He won't need their help in disappointing the people that voted for him, he's started that already by deleting from his website all the "keep the Muslims out" rhetoric that got him elected.

He has, however, kept up his attacks on the free press by blaming them for the "riots" in Portland. At least he is consistent on his hatred of the media, and now he is in a position to do something about it.

In the first few days as President- elect, was his mind on making America great again, or, after the shock had worn off, was his first thought about how much he can increase the room rates at the Trump Hotels?

If we know anything of him, it would be entirely to type if he spent every minute of his time in office dreaming up revenge plots on those who have criticised or crossed or stymied him.

He has had a very public life and we know a lot about him. We know he is a small minded, egotistical, petty, vindictive, self-centred, infantile, pouty, petulant little man with a chip on his shoulder.

It is like America just voted in Biff Tannen, the evil bully from Back to the Future. The baddie just won - that's not how Americans traditionally like their stories to end.

Of course, Hillary actually won - she got more votes than he did but the establishment that wrote the Constitution did not trust the people to elect the President, so they had the people elect members of the elite who would elect the President, and that's how the Democrats won the most votes in 2000 and 2016 but lost both elections.

Trump met the current President for a photo call. The two men could not have looked less alike.

Obama was genial, relaxed and occupied the seat he was sitting in and commanded the room. Trump resembled a child in a high -chair, his feet were touching the floor but still looked like they were swinging. The two chairs were exactly he same, Trump looked lost in his.

Maybe the reality of his position is starting to set in. He is going to have to stop saying the first thing that comes into his head to please an uneducated rabble in front of him and will have to start doing a massive amount of homework, because as President, he will have to start acting like a grown-up.

The Republican machine will know that with a complete newbie in the Whitehouse, they will pretty much be able to do what they want.

What Trump doesn't know can be used to play him like a marionette. The people who decide what to tell him and what to keep from him will be the ones that will really be running America.

Among them will be the right- wing religious types, who will have free reign to concentrate their minds on the genitals of America.

Expect gung-ho attacks on abortion, gays, prostitution - all that above the knee, below the waist stuff that the right is obsessed about.

Meanwhile, their President will be using the power of his office to treat any hot babes around him with the gentlemanly respect for which he is famous.

How did he do it? How did a man become President whose every personality characteristic should have eliminated him from the race?

If he had a proper job, pretty much everything he said in those pantomime call-and-answer rallies would have got him fired.

How could a person who would have been let go as a delivery man get hired to run the richest country on earth?

He tapped into a frustration that "ordinary hard-working people" (Copyright D. Cameron) have about how their lives turned out.

That's why his supporters were mostly old - the young haven't had time to get disappointed yet.

People voted for Trump because their wages had stagnated while their bosses rewarded themselves with all the money that the workers' efforts had created.

They voted for him because for the first time in history their children will be worse off then they are, opportunities are shrinking, jobs are going, the dream has gone.

Two things on that: first, the clue is in the name, it is the American *Dream* - something to hope for, it is not a right, and second, how can anyone really think that a selfish, abusive, fraudulent, cheating, spoiled child of a slum landlord is going to make the lives of the poor better?

Trump is everything that the protest voters were protesting about.

He doesn't pay his taxes, he repeatedly stiffs the people that work for him by refusing to pay them, he uses his wealth to shut down criticism and attack the media through the courts, he is a cheapskate profiteer that sends jobs abroad, shuns American workers and factories and takes public donations intended for charity and buys paintings of himself with them.

When did a man who epitomises the problems in the world become the solution to those problems?

He is not even a very good businessman. He did well with leasing his name on products (made abroad with cheap labour) and self promotion, but is a serial failure at actually running companies, unless you count declaring bankruptcy a success.

His casinos made four trips to the bankruptcy court, because to build them, he borrowed money at such a high interest rate that they were almost bound to fail.

People who owned stock and held bonds in the casinos lost $1.5bn. Trump brags to this day that he personally made a lot of money on them, while putting local contractors and suppliers out of business.

If that sounds like a man who is for the little people, then I am a made in China commemorative Donald Trump bathrobe.

Vladimir Putin and ISIS hailed Trump's victory.

The rest of world is stuck with him and we look forward to his time in office with a certain buttock-clenching alarm.

What will be his top priorities for the first 100 days in office?

First, no-one can wear a tie redder than The Donald's.

Second, blame the media and the Democrats for not going through with all of those things he made up to get votes.

Third, replace the desk in the Oval Office with a stripper pole.

All hail the Pussy Grabber-In-Chief.

Every year I have been putting together the A-Z of the past twelve months with the expert and imaginative help of the listeners to my shows at Christmas and New Year. This is the full and final list for 2016, followed by the same for 2015. It is a list of everything that was on our minds during those years.

They won't be totally faultless. You may find things we missed but at a time when every paper and news show puts together their own lists, I think these are the most complete because they are put together by hundreds of contributors.

Some people and events appear more than once. Some people are known by their first and last names, like Zsa Zsa Gabor, so they appear twice. Some events also have multiple entries.

Think of this like a time capsule. It is what we just went through. We were there when it happened.

A

Died:
AA Gill
Muhammad Ali
Mose Allison - musician
Jean Alexander - actor, Hilda Ogden
Edward Albee - playwright
Joe Alaskey - voice of Bugs Bunny etc after Mel Blanc
Alexis Arquette - actor
Caroline Aherne
Sylvia Anderson - voice of Thunderbirds' Lady Penelope
Ken Adam - production designer Doctor Strangelove, 007 etc
Colonel Abrams - singer
Dalian Atkinson - footballer
Coral Atkins - actor
Signe Anderson - singer Jefferson Airplane
Eric Avebury - founder of Parliamentary Human Rights Group
Richard Adams - author, Watership Down

Article 50
Sam Allardyce,
hired/sacked/hired Anti-semitism
David Attenborough's Planet Earth
2 Mike Ashley
American
elections Alt. Right
Anti-establishment
Aleppo
(Osborne's) Academy schools plan
Adidas withdraws IAAF sponsorship -
doping Anis Amri - Berlin attack
Austerity Apple
iPhone7
Apple refuses to unlock terrorist's
phone Anti-intellectualism
Argos bought by Sainsburys
The Archers domestic abuse plotline
Automatic check-out at Amazon
supermarkets Artificial intelligence
Alsation strangler, Michael Heseltine - did he, didn't he?
Assassination attempt on Nigel Farage, was it, wasn't
it? Alcohol consumption - women catch up with men
Bashar al-Assad
Aid budget
Huma Abedin - Clinton's campaigner
Julian Assange + Wikileaks
Air Force One replacement
cancelled Academy Awards race row
Ankara assassination of Russian
ambassador Austin Reed sold
Arctic oil and gas drilling banned by Obama
Nicola Adams - first British boxer to retain Olympic title,
Rio Ant and Dec - OBE
Lily Allen apologises for Calais Jungle
Admiral Kuznetsov - Russian aircraft carrier in English
Channel Ageing population
American Apparel closes
Asthma medicine required by surprising number of elite
athletes Austrian electors reject far right
Abstract Expressionists at the Royal Academy

B

Died:
David Bowie
John Berry - Beastie Boys

Pete Burns - singer
Prince Buster - singer
Ken Berrie - voice of Postman
Pat Black - singer
Eric Bauersfeld - actor Star Wars "It's a
trap" Kenny Baker - actor R2-D2
Jimmy Bain - rocker, Dio etc
BHS
Lionel Blue - rabbi, broadcaster
Richard Bradford - actor, Man in a
Suitcase Bhumibol Adulyadej - King of
Thailand Boutros Boutros-Ghali
Captain Eric Melrose "Winkle" Brown - flew more types of plane than anyone in
history Pierre Boulez - composer
Anita Brookner - writer, Hotel du Lac

David Bowie Is - V&A's most popular exhibition
ever Boris' blunders
Bake Off
"Battle of the TV Hunks" - tabloid frenzy over Poldark and
Victoria Breibart News
Stephen Bannon
Usain Bolt - wins 9th Olympic
gold Ed Balls dances
Berlin terrorist attack
Brussels terrorist attack
Abu Bakr al-Baghdadi - ISIS leader
The Beckham's kids - tabloids' new
interest Buckingham Palace repairs
Brazilian hairdresser v Article 50 - Deir Dos
Santos British Airways Xmas strike cancelled
Brangelina split
Boko Haram - defeated?
Boaty McBoatface
Alec Baldwin's Trump
impression Black Lives Matter
Billy Bush + Trump +
bus Jeb Bush
Tony Blair comeback - will he/won't he?
Sergeant Alexander Blackman, Marine
A Brexit
Clean brexit Hard
v soft Brexit
"Brexit means Brexit" - Therea May
"Brexit means breakfast" - Andrew Davies, Welsh Conservative
leader Bus advert for Brexit
Big Ben repairs
Blue butterfly thrives in UK after near extinction
Back of the queue - Obama on British? US trade deal if
Brexit Boleyn Ground - West Ham move
Brownlee brothers Olympics - help over the line

Barrel bombs on Aleppo
Blackstar - Bowie
Aaron Banks - UKIP, Brexit
funder Birminham prison riots
Beards
Brazil - Olympics
Byron Burger immigration raid
Adam Barrow - Argos to Gambian President-elect
Eric Bristow - sacked from Sky after child abuse
comments Border controls
Birkini Sepp
Blatter
Tony Blackburn - fired/hired
Bono - Woman of the Year
Bottle flipping craze
David Bridges & Alex Lowe's bodies found in Tibet after 16
years Birther movement - Obama "not born in US"
Bird flu strikes turkey farm at
Xmas Banana Republic shops
close Richard Branson bike crash
Benefits cap
"Breaking Point" - EU leavers' poster
"Britain first" - shouted by Jo Cox's killer
Ken Bone - red sweatered US election debate
questioner Boing stock crash after Trump tweet
"Bigly" - Trump during US election
debate BBC3 moves online

C

Died:
Fidel Castro
Jo Cox
Michael Cimino - director, Deer Hunter etc
Natalie Cole
Leonard Cohen
Ronnie Corbett
Choppers - chimp in PG Tips ad
Johan Cruyff
Phil Chess - Chess records
Dave Cash - DJ
Chapecoense football squad
Charmian Carr - actor, Sound of Music
William Christopher - actor, MASH

Mel C says no to Spice Girls'
reunion David Cameron steps down
Hillary Clinton
"Crooked Hillary"

Jeremy Corbyn re-wins
leadership The cuts (in services)
Cologne New Year sex
attacks Clown craze
Chicago Cubs win World Series
Cuba - US relations "normalised"
Croydon tram crash
Croydon Cat Killer
Chilcot Inquiry
Crystal Meth given to speed up N Korean construction
workers Coup defeated in labour ranks
Cryogenic freezing
Mark Carney - "Britain suffering first lost decade since
1860s" Carrie Fisher heart attack
Calais Jungle
Carrier bag charge
Randy California's estate v Led Zeppelin - Stairway to Heaven
riff Celebrity injunction re. threesome
Child abuse inquiry Cycle
Superhighways Phil
Collins returns Conflict of
interest - Trump Jeremy
Clarkson
Columbia signs peace deal with
Farc China takes US drone
Child refugees - some not
children Bill Cosby
Pauline Cafferkey - Ebola nurse
Kellyanne Conway - Trump strategist
Conkers could vanish - Horse Chestnut Leaf Miner
Church of the Flying Spaghetti Monster recognised in
Netherlands Chewbacca Mom - 164m views and counting
Climate change
Cheerleading at next Olympics
Cheltenham Festival footballers urinate into glass, throw it on
crowd Cincinnati Zoo - gorilla shot
Dominic Chappell - BHS
David Cameron humming at door to No.
10 Climate change - "Chinese plot": Trump
CRISPR Cas9 - gene editing tool
Cheetahs face extinction
Chernobyl Safe Confinement
Arch Camber Sands drownings
Thomas Coville - sets round-the-world solo sailing
record Caudrilla - fracking plans approved
Rochelle Clarke breaks England rugby caps
record Clean for the Queen
Carrier bags charge
Chinese military bases in South China Sea
David Cameran calls Nigeria and Afghanistan "fantastically"
corrupt Channel 4 racing goes to ITV

D

Died:
Paul Daniels
Tony Dyson - special effects designer of R2-D2
etc Michael Delligatti - inventor of Big Mac
Dennis Davis - drummer for
Bowie Frank Dickens - cartoonist
Peter Maxwell Davies -
conductor/composer Patty Duke - actor
Jack Davis - cartoonist Mad magazine
Edward Daly - priest, author, iconic Bloody Sunday
act Patty Duke - actor

Drugs in
prisons Drones
Bob Dylan's Nobel Prize
David Davis, Brexiteer
Drownings - 5000+ refugees
Philip Davis, anti-feminist MP appointed to Equalities
Commission Denmark - happiest, again
The Donald
The Ding Dong Tree - Scottish tree of the
year Rodrigo Duterte's killing spree
Didcot power station disaster
Philip Dilley - Chair of Environment Agency quits after 2015 Xmas
floods Simon Danczuk suspended over sexting
"Drain the swamp" - Trump
Deliveroo + minimum wage
Kirk Douglas - 100 years
old Data eavesdropping
laws Driverless cars
The "deplorables" - Clinton on trump
supporters Dyson's £300 hair dryer
Tom Daley - sets record then eliminated at
Rio Delayed discharge from NHS beds
Petra Kvitova - tennis,
attacked Johnny Depp v
Amber Heard Dab dance craze
Dat boi - internet meme Damn
Daniel - internet meme
Bird landing at Bernie Sanders'
speech Diamond batteries from
nuclear waste Dakota pipeline
Dementia epidemic
Diabetes epidemic
Downing Street cats
Dakota Access Pipeline
Drake - 15 weeks at No 1 in charts

E

Died
Keith Emerson - ELP
Umberto Eco - author
Joe Esposito - Elvis' road manager

Egypt Air Flight 804 crash
Ched Evans' court case
England Rugby team success
England Football team failure
Electoral college - US
elections Recep Erdogan
Emailgate - Clinton
Eugenie and Beatrice denied royal
protection Experts - we've "had our fill"
Entryism - Labour, Republicans
"infiltrated" Elephant decline
Recep Erdogan
EU referendum
The Euro
Euro 2016
Earthquakes - many
Ecuadorian Embassy - Assange still in
there Ecuador cuts Assange's internet feed
Elizabeth Line - Crossrail named
Evil Kermit the Frog - internet meme
Jessica Ennis-Hill retires from athletics
Noel Edmunds' motivational phone service for
cats Ebola epidemic officially over
Easter Rising 100th anniversary
"Enemies of the people" - Daily Mail headline on judges in EU case

F

Died
Dario Fo - playwright
Glenn Frey - The Eagles
Frank Finlay - actor
Margaret Forster - author Georgy Girl
Emile Ford - musician
Rob Ford - crack smoking mayor of Toronto
Carrie Fisher
Tenor Fly - singer

Football child abuse
FIFA corruption
Nigel Farage
Five pound note contains animal fat
Mossack Fonseca leak

Fascism
Chris Froome wins Tour de
france Mo Farah - double double
gold Freedom of movement
Fake news
Far right
Facebook - see entry
above Liam Fox - Brexiteer
Foreign aid
Fallujah
Foxconn replaces 60,000 workers with
robots Food banks
Florida nightclub Pulse
shooting Fake bomb at Old
Traford Harrison Ford injury
fine $2m Fishing rights
"Fantasy Island" - UK stance on
Brexit Fracking
FTSE 100 record high on back of plunging
pound Fabric nightclub closes

G

Died:
Dale Griffin - drummer Mott the Hoople
Christina Grimmie - contestant on US TV's The Voice,
shot Vivean Grey - actor Neighbours
Jon Glenn
AA Gill
David Gest - TV producer, once married Liza
Minnelli Randy Van Gelder - jazz recorder
Reg Grundy - TV producer,
Neighbours Zsa Zsa Gabor
Ron Glass - actor, Barney Miller

Zac Goldsmith
The Grand Tour
Gotthard Base Tunnel - world's longest
opens Goldman Sachs' ex staff fill Trump
cabinet Michael Gove v Boris Johnson and
experts Greek debt crisis
Galileo - European GP satellites operational Ryan
Giggs leaves Manchester Utd after 29 years
Gender fluidity
The Garden Bridge
Grammar schools - PMs
support Giraffes face extinction
Philip Green
Gorilla escapes London
Zoo Gig economy
Gravitational waves discovered

Golf at the Olympics
Google tax bill
Global warming
Bob Geldof v Nigel Farage, battle of the
boats GoPro Karma drones fall from sky
Sigmundur Gunnlaugsson - Iceland PM resigns after Panama Papers
leak Ghostbusters - all female reboot
Rudy Giuliani
Gender identities - New York recognises 31 of them
Geda - Chinese monkey predicts US election result & Euro 2016

H

Died:
Norman Hudis - comedy writer first six Carry On
films Barry Howard - actor, Hi-de-Hi!
Robin Hardy - director, Wicker Man Henry
Heimlich - inventor of the maneuver Zaha
Hadid
Merle Haggard
Harambe - gorilla, shot
Michael Herr - war correspondent, Apocalypse Now
writer Hanoi Hannah - Vietnam War radio personality
Florence Henderson - actor, Brady Bunch
Alan Haven - organist, collaborated with John Barry on Bond
music Donald Henderson - physician, small pox eradication
Guy Hamilton - director, Bond, An Inspector Calls

Hiroshima - first sitting US president
visit Heathrow third runway
Hipsters
Hillsborough disaster Inquest
Bernard Hogan-Howe resigns from Met
Police Hard shoulders disappear on
motorways Hate crime increase after Brexit
Hatchimal - most wanted toy this
Xmas Honey G
Hissene Habre - ex president of Chad
imprisoned HS2
Paul Horner - fake news writer says Trump won due to
him Prince Harry + Meghan Markle
Jerry Hall marries Rupert Murdoch
Hinkley Point C nuclear power
station Hacking
Hero of Cologne - New Year sex
attacks Homelessness
Housing
crisis   House
prices Hillary

Harriet Harman - longest serving female MP
Philip Hamond - Chancellor
Jeremy Hunt - Health Sec v junior doctors
Tom Hiddleston - 007 speculation
Harlequin ladybird invasion
Hospital parking charges
Holloway Prison closed
Hygge - Danish well-being
Jon Hinkley Jr - Reagan shooter released
Hamilton, the musical v Mike Pence

I

Died:
Commander Ian Inskip - Falklands naval officer

Independent newspaper goes online
only Immigration
ISIS
IVF - 3 parent baby
Iceland the country v Iceland the
shop Iceland the football team v
England Ivanka
"Independence day" - Farage on Brexit
vote iPlayer - TV licence now required
iPhone7
ISIS/ISIL
ISS - International Space
Station Zlatan Ibrahimovich
Investigatory Powers Act
Irish government v EU over Apple
tax IDs to vote
Immigration
Istanbul bombing
Israeli settlements
International Criminal Court abandoned by Russia, S. Africa
etc Italian earthquake
Ireland beat All Blacks in
Chicago Indian currency
demonetization Italian debt crisis
Invictus games
Gianni Infantino - new head of FIFA
Eddie Izzard's fetching pink beret and Question
Time Iran economic sanctions lifted by USA
Internet fraud
Idiocracy - no longer a comedy, now a documentary
Insjon, Sweden - laser wielding sex pigs
i360 - attraction opens in Brighton
Illegal settlements in West Bank
Ben Innes selfie with EgyptAir hijacker

Italian referendum on constitutional reform

Caitlyn Jenner "regrets" sex change

J

Died:
Anthony Jay - writer, Yes Minister

Jim - washing machine salesman - Keith Vaz alter-
ego Junior doctors strike
Diane James - UKIP leader for 18
days Juno Jupiter fly-by
Anthony Joshua - IBF heavyweight
title Janet Jackson pregnant at 50
Boris Johnson - Bozo of the FO
JD Sports working conditions
Mick Jagger - father at 73
Deveraux Octavian Basil Jagger.
Jeep Cherokee recall after Anton Yelchin death
Gary Johnson - Libertarian Party nominee, US
elections JAM - just about managing
Jean-Claude
Juncker Jingoism
Jihadi Sid - bouncy castle salesman to ISIS
recruit Brian Johnson leaves AC/DC

K

Died:
Frank Kelly - actor, Father Ted
Andrei Karlov - Russian Ambassador to Turkey,
shot Burt Kwouk - actor, Pink Panther
George Kennedy - actor
Paul Kantner - musician, Jefferson Airplane

King's Cross gentrification
Korea - North v South Kim
Jong-un
Kim Kardashian robbed in Paris
Chris King - first UK double hand
transplant Sadiq Khan - London Mayor
Kittenheels - Theresa May's shoes
Kidlington - ordinary English town magnet for Chinese
tourists Kumbuka - London Zoo's escaped gorilla
Jason Kenny - half of "golden couple" at Rio with Laura
Trott Ku Klux Klan - they're back
Kremlin v US elections
Radovan Karadzic - guilty of war
crimes The Khan family v Trump

L

Died:
Harper Lee - author
Carla Lane - writer Liver Birds, Butterflies, Bread
Tom Leppard - world's most tattooed man
Greg Lake - ELP
John D. Loudermilk - singer, wrote Tobacco Road

"Lock her up" Trump rally chant re. Clinton
Leicester City wins Premier League
Leather trousers - Theresa May's £1000 pair
Andrea Leadsome - having children would "make her a better PM" than
May Dougie Lampkin does wheelie round whole of IoM TT track
Llamas sit in at the Tour de
France "Locker room talk"
Ryan Lochte - "robbed" in Rio
Lord Lucan death certificate
granted Matt LeBlanc - Top Gear
troubles Louisiana floods
"Lyin' Ted Cruz"
Leave (EU)
Christine Lagarde - guilty of
negligence Ladybird books reimagined
Gary Lineker's pants
"The Little People" - politicians' concern
Lego store - world's largest opens in
London Leaves ruin train wheels
Lottery price increase/worse winning
odds Lybia
London Bridge Station revamp
Leaks - PM warns leakers...warning
leaked Legal highs
Alex Lowe & David Bridges' bodies found in Tibet after 16
years Leap second, Dec 31, 2016 23:59:60
Locally sourced food
Land Rover Defender ends
production Leave.EU
Lionheart - Philip Green's yacht
Lynx escapes Dartmoor Zoo
"Lepo" - "what's a Lepo?" top internet search during US eloection debate

M

Died:
Howard Marks - drug dealer, writer, Mr Nice
Ian McCaskill - weatherman
Edgar Mitchell - astronaut
George Martin

George Michael
Scotty Moore - Elvis' guitarist
Gordon Murray - creator Trumpton, Camberwick Green
Garry Marshall - creator Happy Days, director Pretty
Woman Cliff Michelmore - Tv presenter
Michael Massee - actor, Se7en
Nevill Marriner - violinist, conductor
Henry McCullough - musician,
Wings Lonnie Mack - musician

Mannequin challenge
Make America great again
Make Britain great again
Jose Mourinho at Man Utd
Andy Murray wins Wimbledon
Monte dei Paschi - worlds oldest bank
crisis Jose Morinho
Mercury - transit of
Mossack Fonseca
leak Angela Merkel
Meghan Markle + Prince
harry Munich shootings
Theresa May - new
PM Marmitegate
Marzipan pooping pig in Norway
Danielle Muscato - massive Twitter slapdown of Trump
Nicky Morgan v Theresa May's leather trousers
Len Goodman retires from Strictly Come
Dancing Helen Marten - Turner Prize winner
Melania's speech Thomas
Mair - kills Jo Cox Mosul

Len McCluskey - resigns from
Unite Migrant workers
Marine A
Marks and Spencer close
stores Murdoch Sky bid
Ferdinand Marcos, Philippines ex-president buried (died
1989) Elon Musk
Madonna's custody battle for son
Merlin - Alton Towers operator fined over roller-coaster
crash Helen Martin wins Turner Prize
"Mainsteam media"
Muirfield golf club v women
James "Mad Dog" Mattis - named US Defence
Secretary Marijuana legalised in many US states
Moscovium - new element named

N

Died:
Marni Nixon - ghost singer, My Fair Lady, West Side Story etc
Michael Nicholson - war corrspondent
Andy Newman - Thunderclap Newman
Richard Neville - writer, edited Oz magazine
Zara Nutley - actor, Mind Your Language

Robert De Niro v Trump - "I'd like to punch him in the
face" The Night Manager - BBC hit
Nobel Prize in Physics - David J.Thouless, F. Duncan M. Haldane, J. Michael
Kosterlitz Nobel Prize for literature - Bob Dylan
Benjamin Netanyahu v John Kerry, Obama, USA, New Zealand, UN
etc Nice terrorist truck attack
Paul Nuttall - UKIP leader
The Night Manager - TV
hit Night Tube
Negative interest ratesmerlin fined
New Day newspaper
launches/closes Nationalism
Nihonium - new element named Gary

Neville - new England manager

O

Died:
Hugh O'Brian - actor, Life and Legend of Wyatt Earp

Barack Obama
Michelle Obama
Oil price
OPEC
Sarah Olney wins Richmond by-election
Opinion polls get it wrong
Ozone hole in Antarctica shrinks
Ore Oduba wins Strictly Come Dancing
Orgreave - battle of - inquiry ruled out
Olympics
Overseas Aid
Ozzy Osbourne's affair
Oscars race row
Oligarchs
Orangutans on endangered list
George Osborne sacked, still highest earning MP
Offshore banking
Obesity
Georgia O'Keeffe at the Tate
Old Labour returns under Corbyn
Oxfam shop refuses donations of any more 50 Shades of Grey
Oganesson - new element named

P
Died:
Rick Parfitt - musician, Status Quo
Arnold Palmer - golfer
Billy Paul - singer
Jimmy Perry - writer, dad's Army
Prince
Cecil Parkinson - politician
Shimon Peres - ex-Israeli President
Jim Prior - politician
Sylvia Peters - continuity announcer

Popular vote - Hillary won but still
lost Tim Peake - UK astronaut
Planet Earth II
Pastafarians - worshippers at Church of the Flying Spaghetti Monster
recognised Panama Papers
Adam Peaty world records at Rio
Paul Pogba world record transfer to Man
Utd Michael Phelps medal haul continues
Pistol and Boo - Johnny Depp's dogs v
Australia Palace of Westminster repairs
Marine Le Pen
Plain cigarette packaging
Oscar Pistorius appeal fails
Pulse nightclub shootings,
Florida Populism
Patriotism
Pfizer fined £84.2m, overcharging
NHS Pneumonia fells Hillary
Postal service 500 years
old Post Office strike
Poundland price increase
Pound falls post
referendum Prison riots
Pokemon Go
Pearl Harbour first visit by a Japanese
PM Poverty in Uk
Mike Pence US VP
Project Fear - EU
referendum Vladimir Putin
Political correctness (gone
mad) Poppy ban - FIFA
Picasso's Portraits at the National Portrait Gallery
Performance enhancing drugs, especially for
asthma Philippine President Duterte
Post-truth, Oxford dictionary word of the
year Pussy - Trump says he grabs them
Pay for play - Clinton accusation

Giant panda no longer endangered
Pension triple-lock scrapped?
Polymer five pound notes
Beatrix Potter 150th anniversary
Pizzagate - fake news story re. paedophile ring
Port Talbot steelworks

Q

Qantas launches direct London - Australia flights
Quantitative easing
Queen's 90th birthday
Queue - UK at the back of for trade deal: Obama
QI - Fry leaves TV show
Quintuplets born in Australia
Quality Street ditch Toffee Deluxe - Xmas ruined
Quinoa - "food" fad
Quid pro quo - Clinto accusation

R

Died:
Debbie Reynolds
Nancy Reagan
Denise Robertson - broadcaster
Wayne Rogers - actor, "Trapper" John, MASH
Alan Rickman
Brian Rix - actor, President of Mencap
Leon Russell - musician
Vera Rubin - astronomer who confirmed dark matter

Dilma Rousseff - Brazil President impeached
Cliff Richard cleared of abuse charges
Russian state sponsored doping and Olympics
ban Russian hacking of US election
Rio 2016
Rosetta spacecraft crashed on
comet Cristiano Ronaldo wins Ballon
d'Or Remainers
"Remoaners"
Neil Rogers (my hero) inducted posthumously into US Radio Hall of
Fame Nico Rosberg wins F1
Refugees
Rupee - 500 and 1000 notes no longer legal
tender Rio
Royal yacht - new one
mooted Republican Party
Richmond by-election
Rough sleeping
Keith Richards "takes over" BBC4
Claudio Ranieri - manager of Leicesr FC triumph

Russian Ultras - football holiganism at Euros

S
Died:
Garry Shandling - writer, comedian, actor - Larry
Sanders Liz Smith - actor, Royle Family
Martin Stone - guitarist, Pink Fairies, Chilli Willi & the Red Hot Peppers
etc Andrew Sachs - actor, Fawlty Towers
Ed "Stewpot" Stewart - DJ, TV presenter
Peter Shafer - playwright, Amadeus, Equus
Robert Stigwood, entrepreneur, music
mogul Dave Swarbrick - musician
Raine Spencer -
socialite Frank Sinatra Jr
Soptlight - Best Picture Oscar

Syria
Patti Smith accepts Dylan's Nobel Prize, is nervous
Saturday Night Live v Trump
Solar roof tiles - Elon Musk
Martin Shkreli - hikes price of life saving drug 5000%
Southern Rail
Staples shops closing
Ed Sheeran cut by sword by Princess Beatrice
School uniform miscreants sent home
Star Trek 50th anniversary
Shelter - 50th anniversary
Slavery still happening in Britain
Standing Rock protests re. Dakota Access Pipeline
Sex Pistols 40th anniversary
Sugar tax
Sanctions - imposed/lifted - Russia, Iran, Cuba etc
Supreme Court nominations, US
Socialism
Battle of the Somme centenary
Bernie Sanders
Snooper's Charter
Maria Sharapova drugs ban
Schools academies
Simpsons' Trump predictions
Sexting
Alec Salmond
Nicola Sturgeon
Sink holes
Nick Skelton - show-jumper, Rio's oldest gold medalist
Owen Smith - challenged Corbyn for Labour leadership
SpaceX plan to colonise Mars
William Shakespeare - 400th anniversary of death
Samsung phones/tablets catch fire
Supermoon - closest since 1948

T

Died:
Rod Temperton - songwriter, Thriller, Boogie Nights
etc Gareth Thomas - actor, Blake's 7
William Trevor - novelist

Donald J Trump
Trump Tower
Trump University
Trump and Taiwan upset
China Trump's tweets
Trump v Vanity Fair
Trump v Alec Baldwin
Trump v etc etc
Tremendous - Trump's favourite
word Top Gear refurb flop
Laura Trott - half of "golden couple" at Rio with Jason
Kenny Dave Lee Travis - court case
Tsai Ing-wen - Taiwan's first woman
president Transexuals
Tesla cars Insane Mode/Ludicrous
Mode Toblerone redesign
Tate Modern Switch House extension opens - residents
overlooked Tiger numbers rise for 1st time in 100 years
Team GB medal haul in Rio
Trousergate - Theresa May's leather
trousers Traingate - Corbyn v Virgin trains
Yamato Tanooka - Japanese boy, 7, abandoned in bear infested
woods Turkish failed coup
Tennessine - newly discovered
element Two handed transplant -
Britain's first Tube trains run all night
Travel chaos
Liz Truss - first female Lord Chancellor
Thistlecrack - star race horse
TTIP
"Talking Britain down"
Trident renewal
£350m a week for the NHS bus advert
"Take back control" - EU leavers' rallying
cry Tata Steel + Port Talbot
Tsukui Yamayuri En care facility attack, Japan
Carlos Tevez - highest paid athlete in world, £615,000 a week

U

Died:
Lukasz Urban - polish driver killed in Berlin lorry attack

Unilever v Tesco
Ukraine wins Eurovision Song
Contest Underground strike
Unions
Uber
UN Report on UK disability rights
UKIP
Underdog - the year
of US elections
"Unpresidented" - Trump tweet

V

Died:
Boby Vee - singer
Peter Vaughan - actor, Porridge, Game of Thrones
Robert Vaughn - actor, Man from Uncle
Abe Vigoda - actor, Godfather
Viola Beach - band and manager
Vanity - Denise Matthews, singer, Prince
Alan Vega - singer, Suicide (the band)

Volkswagen emissions scandal
Virgin Trains v Jeremy Corbyn
Veil - face cover ban in France
etc Vanity Fair v Trump
Vinyl revival - outsells downloads by
value Vote leave
Vote remain
Virtual reality
Keith Vaz, sex scandal
Vote of no confidence in Jeremy Corbyn
Virtue signalling - internet term re. comments that enhance moral
superiority Max Verstappen - youngest ever F1 winner
Video recorders - last known manufacturer stops production
"Vi coactus" - Dianne James signs UKIP leadership papers "under duress"

W

Died:
Gene Wilder
Terry Wogan
Victoria Wood
Papa Wemba - singer
Michael White - producer, Rocky Horror Show, Monty Python
etc Maurice White - Earth Wind and Fire
Duke of Westminster
Alan Williams - Beatles' first manager

Tony Warren - screenwriter, Coronation Street
Andrzej Wajda - film director
Bobby Wellins - musician

Wales' football team reach first semi-final of major tournament
Max Whitlock - first British gymnast to win Olympic gold
Wall - big, beautiful, Mexico paying
Wooden plates in restaurants
Bradley Wiggins retires from cycling
Steven Woolfe - UKIP MEP, altercation with UKIP MEP Mike
Hookem Danny Willett wins Masters golf tournament
John Whittingdale MP+ sex worker = sacked
Steven Woolfe - UKIP leadership contender hospitalised by UKIP
MEP W.H.O. declares Zika outbreak over
"What is the EU" internet search spike after
referendum Wikileaks
Anthony Weiner's emails rock Clinton campaign
Geert Wilders - Dutch politician's hate speech
trial Wallonia v Canada-EU trade deal
Winchester - "best place to live in UK"
"We're here because we're here" Jeremy Deller art project, 100 anniv Battle of
Somme Kanye West
"Whinge-orama" - Boris Johnson on EU referendum debate

X

Xenophobia
Xi Jinping

Y
Died:
Anton Yelchin - actor, Star Trek
Alan Young - Mr Ed etc
The Young Pope - TV series
Yorkshire Ripper moved back to jail
Jimmy Young - DJ, singer
Yahoo confirm they were hacked in 2013/14

Operation Yew Tree
Yazidis persecuted by ISIS
Yemen
Yulin dog meat festival

Z

Died:
Zsa Zsa Gabor
Zaha Hadid
Vilos Zsigmond - cinematographer, Close Encounters, Deer Hunter

Zero hours contracts
Zero interest rates

Zafira cars
recalled Zika virus
Zionism - Ken Livingstone said Hitler supported
it Zack Goldsmith loses Richmond by-election

2015

A
Aurora Borealis visible as far south as
Norfolk Apple Watch
Apple music
streaming Adele
Airspace invasion (Turkey v Russia, Russia v UK
etc) Airport expansion
Storm Abigail: first storm of Met Office "Name our Storms"
project Bashar al-Assad
Carlos Acosta retires
Astronaut Tim Peake
Airbus crash in Alps
Ashley Maddison
Dianne Abbott + Jeremy Corbyn + field
=? Austerity (still)
Android overtakes Apple operating system in
sales Air show disasters
Amazon's efficient tax affairs
The Ashes: English victory
Accident and Emergency crisis
Tony Abbott ousted in Aus
Julian Assange still in there
Al Qaeda outcrazied by ISIS
Afghanistan – West's gains wiped
out Roman Abramovich loses
patience Alton Towers Disaster
Assemble the architecture collective wins the Turner
Prize Appleby floods
"Are you alright?" Paxman to
Miliband Shaker Aamer released
Arctic oil and gas exploration
Anonymous v ISIS
Armed police
Lord Ashcroft
Ai Weiwei exhibition at
RA Antibiotic resistance
King Abdullah, Saudi Arabia (d)
Alphabet – Google's new holding company
Lucy Allen MP "unless you die" Tweet addition
allegation Mike Allen (d)
Athleisurewear
Address Hotel fire, Dubai

B
Cilla Black (d)
BT Tower briefly reopens for 50th
anniversary Sepp Blatter
Le Bataclan
Simon Brodkin throws fake cash at Sepp Blatter = a pic of the
year Big banks earn billions, don't pay tax
Bees – colony collapse
disorder Errol Brown (d)
Rebecca Brooks innocent!
FC Barcelona – European Champions
(again) Natalie Bennett + Nick Ferrari = car
crash Brexit
Hilary Benn's let's go to more war
speech The Beatles join streaming
services Justin Bieber
Buy-to-let tax
changes Beards
Back to the Future – the future is
now! Yogi Berra (baseball) (d)
Bishop (first female C of E)
Jenson Button marriage
Jenson Button marriage
over Chuck Blazer
whistleblower Benefit cuts
Black cabs v Uber Beach
body ready advert
Camila Batmangshjshoiduqodklshbldjh
Andy Burnham also ran
Ed Balls loses seat
Bobby Kristina Brown (d)
Bitter Lake – Adam Curtis film straight to
iPlayer Bohemian Rhapsody 40 years old
Tony Blair insists he was right all
along Leon Brittan (d)
Bridge Over You No1 at Xmas
Usain Bolt confirms he's the
fastest Birdman best picture Oscar
Abu Bakr al-Baghdadi
Boko Haram
Bobby Kristina Brown
(d) Blood moons
Joy Beverley, Beverley Sisters (d)
Russell Brand "retires from
politics" Mhairi Black youngest MP
David Black, singer, Goldie (d) Blue
Moon diamond sells for £33m
"Bulbous salutation" - Morrissey wins Bad Sex in Fiction
Award Black spider memos of Prince Charles released
John Beeden sets non-stop solo Pacific row
record John Bradbury Specials drummer (d)
Bananatastrophe (banana blight)

Bulldog on skateboard travels under 30 people, sets
record Bangkok bomb in shrine
Pamela Cundell, actor
(d) Storm Barney
Peter Baldwin, actor (d)

C
Jeremy Clarkson
Coalition (d) Call
Clegg (d)
Benedict Cumberbatch's Hamlet
Douglas Carswell v Uncle
Nige Ted Cruz
Princess Charlotte
Caudrilla fracking plans near Blackpool
rejected Coal mine closure
Daniel Craig "rather slash my wrists than play Bond
again" Chelsea FC fans' racist chant
David Cameron and the porcine initiation
allegation The Cycle Superhighway
Jackie Collins (d)
Cadbury's Cream Egg recipe
change Lady C
Charlie Hebdo Cumbrian
floods (again) Child tax
credit changes Carrier
bags = 5p Jeremy
Corbyn wins...
Corbynmania follows
Yvette Cooper also
ran C3PO returns
Cecil the lion (d)
Cilla Black (d)
Cuba US relations
thaw Vince cable loses
seat Hilary Clinton
George Cole (d)
Cyber hacking
Wes Craven (d)
The Croydon cat killer
Chilcot Report (still
waiting) Lewis Collins,
actor (d) Climate talks
Conservative general election
victory Victorina Chua (poisoning
nurse) Church of England ad
banned Duchess of Cambridge
gives birth Ornette Coleman (d)
Crossrail disruption
Ben Carson Republican hopeful
Confederate flag removed from public buildings in
US Calais migrant crisis

Child sex abuse
Conservative party bullying scandal Lyntom
Crosby Tory election "mastermind"
Sebastien Coe denies ethics charges
Bill Clinton's old home
burns The Cereal Cafe
Cameron's "brain fade" over favourite team: Aston Villa or West
Ham "Call me Dave" book revelations
Clock US student brought to school – not a
bomb Bill Cosby sex allegations
CamJet – Cameron getting own
plane Clapping in Commons (SNP)
Cow dung patties "sell like hot cakes"

Chinese corruption crackdown

D
Davis Cup – GB win
Novak Djokovic wins Wimbledon
Dippy the diplodocus moved from the Natural History
Museum Daesh
Storm Desmond
Drones
Robert Dyas gay/straight Xmas
ad Dart Vader
Downton Abbey (d)
Peter Donaldson newsreader (d)
Peter Dimmock first Grandstand presenter
(d) Michael Dean broadcaster (d)
Jim Diamond singer (d)
Diamond – world's second largest found in
Botswana Doctors' strike that didn't happen
Doping in sport
Diesel police dog killed by Paris
terrorists Dec married (not to Ant)
Dancing man fat shamed
Dismaland by Banksy
Discount supermarkets rising market
share Rachel Dolezal black or white?
Baroness D'Souza keeps cab waiting while she sees opera – charges
us Data breaches
Driverless vehicles
Devolution
Val Doonican (d)

E
Albert Einstein – 100 years of general relativity
Eagles Of Death Metal
Ebola
Elephant poaching
Egypt terrorist attack
UEFA back President Michel Platini
Storm Eva

The Ed Stone (a goof too far for
Miliband) The EU
Everest moves 3cm southwest after Nepal
earthquake Anita Ekberg (d)
Jack Ely (Louie Louie singer)
(d) eBay 20 years old
EU renegotiation
Elephant and Castle new layout
chaos Mohammed Emwazi (Jihadi
John) (d) ELO return
El Capitan , Yosemite scaled by free
climbers Elm Street Guest House

F
FA withdraw Michel Platini
support The Force Awakens
Tyson Fury
Flooding
Fracking
Tim Farron
Fifty Shades of grey film
released FIFA corruption
Foo Fighters cancel Glasto
Freedom of Information Act under
attack Nigel Farage v Douglas Carswell
Fox hunting debate continues
FHM magazine "suspends
publication" Flight MH370
Falcon 9 takes off and lands
Florence and the Machine step in for Foo Fighters at
Glasto Forex scandal
Food banks
Colin Fry spiritualist (d)
Chris Froome wins Tour de
France False widow spiders
Falling off stage: Dave Grohl, The Edge, Harry
Styles Andy Fraser, bassist with Free (d)
Face transplant – world's first
full Fat tax
Brian Friel, dramatist
(d) Francois Hollande
Mo Farah triple
double Ferguson riots
French train attack foiled
Michele Ferrero chocolate magnate
(d) Forth Road Bridge closed
Frostbit boy goes viral

G
Bear Grylls and Oback Arama
Greek debt
Greek islands + immigrants

GREXIT
Paul Gascoigne still drinking+harassing ex-
girlfriend Germanwings crash
GCHQ's spying
Guantanamo
Green Party: General election 1.1m votes = 1
MP Gun crime in USA
Gold/blue dress that broke the
internet Global warming
Germaine Greer upsets transgender
women Great British Bake Off
The Garden Bridge on the Thames
Dave Grohl: "I think I just broke my
leg" Gulls attack
Alberto Giacometti's Pointing Man most expensive sculpture
$141m Ryan Giggs, Gary Neville allow homeless to stay in hotel
Guru Josh, rave pioneer (d)
Joaquin "El Chapo" Guzman, drug lord, escapes

H
Hazel Holt novelist (d)
House of Lords reform
Don Howe, footballer (d)
Helicopter crash in New
Zealand Lewis Hamilton F1 win
Lenny Henry/Ainsley Harriet mix
up Hiroshima 70th anniversary
Jimmy Hill, footballer (d)
Hawker Hunter crash at
Shoreham Hatton Garden heist
Hoverboards
Steve Harvey crowns wrong Miss
Universe Harriet Harman briefly Labour
leader Jeremy Hunt v NHS
Gordon Honeycombe, newsreader (d)
William Hague retires to Upper House
Homeland TV show Arabic graffiti
incident Heathrow expansion
Hacked
Off HS2
Prince Harry + Pippa
Middleton? Hungarian fence
Heysel stadium disaster 30th anniversary
Peter Hain: critic of the Lords becomes
Lord Hydrogen Fuel Cell
Hyper Cacher
attack Hipsters
Geoffrey Howe (d)
Hoegh Osaka cargo ship carrying luxury cars grounded in
Solent Keith Harris (d)
Dennis Healey
(d) Katie Hopkins

Hiccups – small boy gets through Australian national
anthem Hoax caller to Cameron "off my face"
"Hell yes, I'm tough enough" (Miliband)

I
Ireland legalises gay marriage
Interest rate rise in US
Instagram reaches 400m users
Iranian nuclear agreement
Indian PM Modi visits UK + Pakistan
International Space Station
ISIS
Immigration
Indian nuclear deal with Russia
"I have got a huge cold" Natalie Bennett excuses performance on Nick Ferrari
show Identity theft
Internet Explorer (d) In/out
referendum Independent
Living fund (d) Islamsists

J
Caitlyn Jenner
Boris Johnson flattens 10 year old in "friendly" rugby
match The Jungle, Calais
"Jez we can"
Lord Janner (d)
Elton John gets call from
"Putin" Japan v whales
Jihadi John (d)
Je suis Charlie
Junior   doctors   don't
strike   Lisa   Jardine
historian (d) Juicers
Wilko Johnson did not die

K
Alyan Kurdi
Liz Kendall also ran
Kids Company
Korea N v S
B.B. King (d)
Ben E King (d)
Kim Jong-un's haircut
Charles Kennedy (d)
Kunduz, Afghanistan, hospital airstrike
Anne Kirkbride (Corrie) (d)
Jurgen Klopp takes over at Liverpool FC
Koh-i-noor diamond – India still wants it back
Kellingley Colliery (d)
Harry Kane – the real thing
Kale

Kinks – Ray and Dave reunite
Kepler 452b – habitable planet found: Earth 2.0
Ellsworth Kelly, artist (d)
Imran Khawaja, jihadist who missed moisturiser
Mount Kinabalu strippers

L
Princess Leia
Leicester City FC
Stephen Lewis ("I 'ate you Butler!")
(d) Lesbos immigrant crisis
Robert Loggia actor (d)
Frank Lampard marries Christine
Bleakley Low tax jurisdictions
Jonah Lomu (d)
Libby Lane – first female bishop
Robert Lewandowski – 5 goals in 9
minutes Lottery rule change
James Last (d)
Lord Lucan's son applies for death
certificate Jerry Lee Lewis' farewell tour
Leytonstone stabbing ("This is for
Syria") Christopher Lee (d)
Lego shortage
Meadowlark Lemon, Harlem Globetrotter
(d) Lemmy reached Hammersmith, sleeps
(d) London Cycle Hire Scheme re-brand
"Long term economic plan": Tories favourite phrase
Oliver Letwin apolgises over 1985 comments
Andreas Lubitz, co-pilot, crashed Germanwings Flight 4U9525
(d) Lee Kuan Yew, Singapore's first PM (d)

M
Angela Merkel's immigration policy
Angela Merkel - Time magazine's person of the
year Andy Murray – best personality!
Ed Miliband also ran
Dave Mackay footballer
(d) Elon Musk
Mansion tax
Many Clouds wins Grand
National Maureen O'Hara (d)
Madonna falls at the Brits
Shane MacGowan's new
teeth Madonna v son at Xmas
Jose Morinho – not so special this
year Henning Mankell writer (d)
Ron Moody (d)
Market rigging banking fines
Ed Miliband's spare kitchens
Ed Miliband's kitchen interview with Russell
Brand Milibabes

Mosul, Afghanistan, falls to ISIS
Al Murray v Nigel Farage
Kellie Maloney
Albert Maysles documentary film maker (d)
Patrick Macnee (d)
Metrojet Flight 9268 crash
Million Mask March
Miss Universe mix up
Olly Murs X-Factor mix up
Barry Manilow marries
Ewan MacColl singer songwriter (d)
Migration crisis
Mytholmroyd floods
Floyd Mayweather beats Manny Pacquiao
Zayn Malik leaves One Dimension
Nicki Minaj v Taylor Swift Twitter spat
Michael Meacher, politician (d)
Narendra Modi, Indian PM visits UK
Warren Mitchell (d)
Mali hotel attack
Milk price row
Muscle dysmorphia
Al Molinaro, Happy Days actor (d)
Rupert Murdoch + Jerry Hall
Alexander McQueen at the V&A
Magna Carta 800 years anniversary

N
Nepal earthquake
Leonard Nimoy (d)
National Police Air Service tweet spycam Michael McIntyre
pic Viv Nicholson ("Spend , spend, spend") (d)
New Zealand win Rugby World Cup
David Nobbs (Reginald Perrin writer) (d)
Nurses – foreign ones must earn £35,000 or they're
out NHS charity song
Nuclear deal with
China Night Tube
Boris Nemtsov, Russian opposition leader
(d) Queen Nefertiti's tomb found?
New Horizons space probe encounters Pluto
Nauru island, Australian migrant detention
centre Nigella's avocado on toast
National Living Wage
Nudge theory
Northern powerhouse
Nuclear button – Corbyn won't press
it New Zealand's new flag referendum
Nazi gold train found?
National anthem: Corbyn does not sing, then sings

O

Operation stack on M20
One child policy in China changes to two child policy
George Osborne, next Tory leader?
Oldham West and Royton by-election – Corbyn's first test
Olympic doping
Jamie Oliver v sugar – sugar wins
Obesity
Overseas Aid
Organ donation opt-out policy in Wales
Odense Zoo, Denmark, dissects lion
Operation Yewtree
OPEC floods market with oil
Oil price drops
Oklahoma police shooting
Victor Orban, Hungarian PM refuses to accept migrants
Mesut Osil, footballer of the year?

P
Paris terrorist attack
Ronnie Pickering (do you know who I
am?) Pink bus (Harriet Harman's)
Palace of Westminster repair
bill Vladimir Putin
Terry Pratchett (d)
Palmyra destruction
Walter Palmer lion
killer Petrol under £1
Pablo Picasso's Women of Algiers Version O most expensive painting
$179m Oscar Pistorius guilty of murder
Processed meats WHO cancer
alert PMQ's: Corbyn's makeover
Poppies – ceramic on sale and on
tour Michel Platini banned from
football Palmyra
Peshmerga
The Privy Council + Corbyn
Pollsters get it wrong on general
election Playboy abandons nudity
Polish PM says no to migrant benefits
demand Lance Percival (d)
Premier League's unpredictable
season Jimmy Page v Robbie Williams
Plastic banknotes launched
Cynthia Payne (d)
Poonado – whale deals with pesky divers
Police refuse to investigate odd numbered house
burglaries Charlotte Proudman v Linkedin sexism
Pistol and Boo, Australia v Johnny Depp's illegal
dogs Paolo Porpora £1m painting holed by child
Prosecco overtakes champagne in sales value
Prince Philip: "Just take the f****** picture"

Q
The Queen becomes longest reigning monarch
The Queen's fur coat
Quantitative easing
Quinoa "superfood"
Quality Street shrinks
Queer gender politics
Qatar World Cup scandal
Quid – new pound coin shape introduced

R
Brendan Rogers ex Liverpool
manager Warren Mitchell (d)
Demis Roussos
(d) R2D2
Michele Ferrero chocolate magnate (d)
Wayne Rooney all-time England goal
record Ruth Rendell (d)
Cecil Rhodes' plaque and statue under
attack Robot panic
Rhodes colossus planned
Lionel Richie ruled Glastonbury
Eddie Redmayne wins best actor Oscar
Johnny Rockard Ukip's pornstar
candidate Richard III reburial
Joe Root – world's best batsman?
"Run and hide, don't play dead" – security advice for terrorist
attack Rugby World Cup
Susanna Reid flirts
Republican TV debates
Malcolm Rifkind cash for access
allegations Renewables funding U-turn
Rico Rodriguez, trombonist(d)

S
Charlie Sheen HIV+
SeaWorld crisis caused by Black
Fish Han Solo
Luke Skywalker
"So called" Islamic
State Omar Sharif (d)
"Swarm" - Cameron on migrants
Lord John Buttifant Sewel + drugs + prostitutes = no
surprise Strictly Come Dancing top rated TV show of 2015
Martin Shkreli ups price of HIV drug by
5000% Martin Shkreli arrested for fraud
Harry Styles -constant press
presence Spectre
Oliver Sacks, neurologist, author
(d) Sangin, Afghanistan, falls to
Taliban Steve Strange (d)
Sousse, Tunisia Islamist attack

Pavel Srnicek, footballer
(d) Syria
Syriza win Greek
election Brian Sewel (d)
Helmut Schmidt (d)
Striped red paint job on Chelsea
house Sinkholes
Frank Sinatra 100 anniversary
Pete Seeger (d)
Steel industry crisis
Nicola Strugeon
Star Wars
Percy Sledge (d)
Bernie Sanders Republican
hopeful Saudi Arabia oil war
Saudi Arabia allows women's
vote Taylor Swift
Chris Squire, bassist
(d) Sugar tax
Streaming music income overtakes
download Shoreham Airshow disaster
Max Schrems v Facebook over data
privacy Hugh Scully (d)
Terry Sue-Patt, actor (d)
Shawshank Redemption-style prison breakout in
NY Peter Sutcliffe "no longer mentally ill"
"Silent bomber" couple jailed
Jack Straw cash for access allegations
Grant Shapps second job as web
marketer Nicholas Smith, actor (Mr
Rumbold) (d) Saint Mother Teresa
Space X's reusable
rockets Stop The War's
Xmas party Scottish
National Party Spiralizers
"Surgical strikes"
Stolen Stradivarius violin recovered

T Transexuals
Donald Trump

Twitter troll "clampdown"
Top Gear (d)
Alex Tsipris Greek PM
Tax Credit cuts U-turn
Transatlantic Trade and Investment
Partnership Justin Trudeau, new Canadian PM
Talk Talk data breach
Tesco's travails
Phil Taylor, drummer
(d) Tunisian attacks
Aiden Turner, scythes in Poldark

Thomas Cook "breached duty of care" over Corfu
deaths Third runway at Heathrow?
Margaret Thatcher's possessions
auctioned TFL v black cabbies
"Tampon tax"
Jackie Trent, singer-songwriter
(d) Troops sued by Taliban
Twinkle, singer (d)

U
Umpqua Community College shooting
UKIP: General election 3.8m votes = 1
MP Uber
USS Theodore Roosevelt too big for Portsmouth
Underground strikes + overnight service
UCAS to enforce blind-name applications to tackle race
bias UN approves Syria resolution
Universal
Credit Ukraine
Miss Universe mix
up UEFA corruption
Unicyclist freed from under bus in Walthamstow
U2 cancel Paris gig, then perform
Ultra Low Emission Zone confirmed for 2020
Chuka Umunna signs up for Labour leadership battle

Chuka Umunna withdraws from Labour leadership battle

V
Volkswagen emissions
scandal Vaping
Jamie Vardey breaks Premier League goal scoring record
Yanis Varoufakis motorbiking Greek finance minister
VE Day 70th anniversary
VJ Day 70th anniversary
The vinyl revival
Virtual reality
Vulcan bomber retired
Vegan shadow environment minister
VAT savings at airport shops not passed on

W
World War 2 ends - 70th anniversary
Tom Watson – campaigner or bully?
Kanye West says he'll run for president
Kanye West: "You are watching the greatest living rock star on the
planet"!! Saint West: baby to Kanye and Kim
Tim Wonnacott suspended from Bargain Hunt
"We've had a mammary lapse" - The Sun briefly retires Page
3 Water on Mars
Water cannon ban (Boris upset)
Chris Woodhead, educationalist
(d) Weather extremes

Whale vomit found on beach sells for £11,000
Colin Welland "The British are coming" writer
(d) Weasel takes a ride on a woodpecker
Max Whitlock first GB gymnast to win World Championship
gold Palace of Westminster repair bill
Louis Walsh sacked/not sacked from X
Factor Water cannon use ruled out by
Theresa May Windows 10
Wealth inequality
Arsene Wenger Premier League's longest serving manager
Wales through to Euro 2016 - first major football tournament since
1958 Trevor Ward-Davies, bassist (d)
Stevie Wright, The Easybeats pop star (d)

X
Xmas No1 = NHS
Xi Jinping state visit
Xylella fastidiosa – olive tree blight

Y
Operation Yewtree
Alan Yentob
Pauline Yates, actor (d)
Yulin dog meat festival

Z
Zoo magazine "suspends publication"
Zhang Ziyi Chinese actress gives birth
Mark Zuckerberg announces wealth giveaway
Mark Zuckerberg becomes father
Zero hours contracts
Zito, footballer (d)

Printed in Great Britain
by Amazon